Spanish
phrase book

D1460921

AA Publishing

Contents

English edition prepared by First Edition Translations Ltd, Great Britain

Designed and produced by AA Publishing

First published in 1995 as Wat & Hoe Spaans, © Uitgeverij Kosmos bv - Utrecht/Antwerpen

Van Dale Lexicografie bv - Utrecht/Antwerpen

This edition © Automobile Association Developments Limited 1997
Reprinted 1997
Reprinted Jun and Sep 1998
Reprinted May and Oct 1999
Reprinted Feb and Sep 2000
Reprinted Apr and Sep 2001
Reprinted Feb and Aug 2002
Reprinted Feb 2003, Jul 2003 and Sep 2003
Reprinted Dec 2003, May and Aug 2004
Reprinted Apr, May and Aug 2005

A CIP catalogue record for this book is available from the British Library

Published by AA Publishing (a trading name of Automobile Association Developments Limited, whose registered office is Southwood East, Apollo Rise, Farnborough, Hampshire GU14 0JW. Registered number 1878835).

A02775

Typeset by Anton Graphics Ltd, Andover, Hampshire.

Printed and bound in Italy by Printer Trento S.r.l.

Find out more about AA Publishing and the wide range of services the AA provides by visiting our website at www.theAA.com/bookshop

Introduction

● **Welcome to the AA's Spanish Phrasebook, which contains everything you'd expect from a comprehensive language guide. It's concise, accessible and easy to understand, and you'll find it indispensable on your trip abroad.**

The guide is divided into 15 themed sections and starts with a pronunciation table which explains the phonetic pronunciation to all the words and phrases you'll need to know for your trip, while at the back of the book is an extensive word list and grammar guide which will help you construct basic sentences in Spanish.

Throughout the book you'll come across coloured boxes with a 🌏 beside them. These are designed to help you if you can't understand what your listener is saying to you. Hand the book over to them and encourage them to point to the appropriate answer to the question you are asking.

Other coloured boxes in the book – this time without the symbol – give alphabetical listings of themed words with their English translations beside them.

For extra clarity, we have put all English words and phrases in black, foreign language terms in red and their phonetic pronunciation in italic.

This phrasebook covers all subjects you are likely to come across during the course of your visit, from reserving a room for the night to ordering food and drink at a restaurant and what to do if your car breaks down or you lose your traveller's cheques and money. With over 2,000 commonly used words and essential phrases at your fingertips you can rest assured that you will be able to get by in all situations, so let the AA's Spanish Phrasebook become your passport to a secure and enjoyable trip!

Pronunciation table

The pronunciation provided should be read as if it were English, bearing in mind the following main points:

Vowels

Vowels in Spanish are very open

a	is like **a** in amber,	*ah*	as in **casa**	*kahsah*
e	is like **e** in egg,	*eh*	as in **esta**	*ehstah*
i	is like **ee** in seen,	*ee*	as in **isla**	*eeslah*
o	is like **o** in John,	*oh*	as in **hotel**	*ohtehl*
u	is like **oo** in room,	*oo*	as in **uno**	*oonoh*
y	is like **ee** in seen,	*ee*	as in **y**	*ee*
	the diphthong **ay** is pronounced as in aisle or eye			
			as in **hay**	*eye*

Consonants

Consonants are as in English, pronounced less clearly, except

b/v	are pronounced roughly the same		
		as in **vamos**	*bahmohs*
c	before e and i is soft and is like the **th** in tha**th**		
		as in **la acera**	*lah ahthehrah*
	before a,o and u is hard		
		as in **cosa**	*kohsah*
cu	before another vowel is pronounced like **cw**		
		as in **la cuenta**	*lah kwehntah*
g	before e and i is soft and is like the Scottish **ch** in lo**ch**,		
		as in **la gente**	*lah <u>h</u>ehnteh*
	before a, o and u is hard		
		as in **gato**	*ghahtoh*
gu	before e and i is pronounced as hard **g**		
		as in **la guía**	*geeah*
	before a, o and u is pronounced like **gw**		
		as in **guapo**	*gwahpoh*
gü	before e and i is pronounced like **gw**		
		as in **lingüística**	*leengwees-teekah*
h	is silent		
j	is like the soft **g**	as in **jarra**	*hahrrah*
ll	is like **lli** in billion	as in **llave**	*lyahbeh*
ñ	is like **ni** in onion	as in **año**	*ahnyoh*
r	is rolled as in the Scottish **r**, **rr** is a longer roll		
z	is like **th** in thought	as in **taza**	*tahthah*

The stress normally falls on the last syllable of the word (**hotel**), except that words ending in a vowel (not including **y**) or in n or s (**casa, casas**) are stressed on the next to the last syllable. All exceptions are indicated by a written acute accent (**Córdoba**, *kohrdohbah*).

Note: In the south, the soft **c** and the **z** are pronounced *s*. This is also true in Latin America.

Useful lists

Useful lists

1 Useful lists

1.1 Today or tomorrow?

What day is it today? _____	¿Qué día es hoy?
	keh deeah ehs oy?
Today's Monday_____	Hoy es lunes
	oy ehs loonehs
– Tuesday_____	Hoy es martes
	oy ehs mahrtehs
– Wednesday _____	Hoy es miércoles
	oy ehs myehrkohlehs
– Thursday_____	Hoy es jueves
	oy ehs hooehbehs
– Friday_____	Hoy es viernes
	oy ehs byehrnehs
– Saturday _____	Hoy es sábado
	oy ehs sahbahdoh
– Sunday _____	Hoy es domingo
	oy ehs dohmeengoh
in January _____	en enero
	ehn ehnehroh
since February _____	desde febrero
	dehsdeh fehbrehroh
in spring_____	en primavera
	ehn preemahbehrah
in summer_____	en verano
	ehn behrahnoh
in autumn _____	en otoño
	ehn ohtohnyoh
in winter_____	en invierno
	ehn eenbyehrno
1997_____	mil novecientos noventa y siete
	meel nohbehthyentohs nohbehntah ee
	syehteh
the twentieth century _____	el siglo XX (veinte)
	ehl seegloh beheenteh
What's the date today? ___	¿Qué día es hoy?
	keh deeah ehs oy?
Today's the 24th_____	Hoy es 24 (veinticuatro)
	oy ehs beheenteekwahtroh
Monday 3 November _____	lunes 3 (tres) de noviembre de 1998 (mil
1998	novecientos noventa y ocho)
	loonehs trehs deh nohbyehmbreh deh meel
	nohbehthyehntohs nohbehntah ee ohchoh
in the morning _____	por la mañana
	pohr lah mahnyahnah
in the afternoon _____	por la tarde
	pohr lah tahrdeh
in the evening _____	por la noche
	pohr lah nohcheh
at night_____	por la noche
	pohr lah nohcheh
this morning _____	esta mañana
	ehstah mahnyahnah

this afternoon _____	esta tarde
	ehstah tahrdeh
this evening _____	esta noche
	ehstah nohcheh
tonight _____	esta noche
	ehstah nohcheh
last night _____	anoche
	ahnohcheh
this week _____	esta semana
	ehstah sehmahnah
next month _____	el mes próximo
	ehl mehs prohxeemoh
last year _____	el año pasado
	ehl ahnyo pahsahdoh
next... _____	el/la... próximo/a
	ehl/lah... prohxeemoh/ah
in...days/weeks/ _____ months/years	dentro de...días/semanas/meses/años
	dehntroh deh...
	deeahs/sehmahnahs/mehsehs/ahnyohs
...weeks ago _____	hace...semanas
	ahthe...sehmahnahs
day off _____	día libre
	deeah leebreh

🕐 .2 Bank Holidays

● **The most important** Bank Holidays in Spain are the following:

January 1	New Year's Day (Año Nuevo)
January 6	Epiphany (Epifanía)
March 19	St. Joseph's Day (San José)
March/April	Good Friday (Viernes Santo)
March/April	Easter Monday(Catalonia) (Lunes Santo)
May 1	Labour Day (Día del Trabajo)
May/June	Corpus Christi (Corpus Christi)
July 25	St. James's Day (Santiago)
August 15	Assumption Day (Asunción)
October 12	Columbus Day (Día de las Américas)
November 1	All Saints' Day (Todos los Santos)
December 6	Constitution Day (Día de la Constitución)
December 8	Immaculate Conception (Inmaculada Concepción)
December 25	Christmas (Navidad)

There are also various regional holidays like San Fermín in Pamplona (July 6-13) and the Fallas in Valencia (March 19).

🕐 .3 What time is it?

What time is it? _____	¿Qué hora es?
	keh ohrah ehs?
It's nine o'clock _____	Son las nueve
	sohn lahs nwehbeh
– five past ten _____	Son las diez y cinco
	sohn lahs dyeth ee theenkoh
– a quarter past eleven _____	Son las once y cuarto
	sohn lahs ohntheh ee kwahrtoh
– twenty past twelve _____	Son las doce y veinte
	sohn lahs dohthe ee beheenteh

– half past one _____	Es la una y media	*ehs lah oonah ee mehdyah*
– twenty–five to three_____	Son las tres menos veinticinco	*sohn lahs trehs mehnohs beheenteetheenkoh*
– a quarter to four_____	Son las cuatro menos cuarto	*sohn lahs kwahtroh mehnohs kwahrtoh*
– ten to five _____	Son las cinco menos diez	*sohn lahs theenkoh mehnohs dyehth*
– twelve noon_____	Son las doce del mediodía	*sohn lahs dohtheh dehl mehdyohdeeah*
– midnight _____	Son las doce de la noche	*sohn lahs dohtheh deh lah nohcheh*
half an hour _____	media hora	*mehdyah ohrah*
What time? _____	¿A qué hora?	*ah keh ohrah?*
What time can I come ____ round?	¿A qué hora puedo pasar?	*ah keh ohrah pwehdoh pahsahr?*
At... _____	A las...	*ah lahs...*
After... _____	Después de las...	*dehspwehs deh lahs...*
Before... _____	Antes de las...	*ahntehs deh lahs...*
Between...and... _____	Entre las...y las...	*ehntreh lahs...ee lahs...*
From...to... _____	De las...a las...	*deh lahs...ah lahs...*
In...minutes _____	Dentro de...minutos	*dehntroh deh...meenootohs*
– an hour _____	Dentro de una hora	*dehntroh deh oonah ohrah*
– ...hours _____	Dentro de...horas	*dehntroh deh...ohrahs*
– a quarter of an hour ____	Dentro de un cuarto de hora	*dehntroh deh oon kwahrtoh deh ohrah*
– three quarters of_____ an hour	Dentro de tres cuartos de hora	*dehntroh deh trehs kwahrtohs deh ohrah*
early/late _____	muy temprano/tarde	*mwee tehmprahnoh/tahrdeh*
on time_____	a tiempo	*ah tyehmpoh*
summer opening hours___	horario de verano	*ohrahryoh deh behrahnoh*
winter opening hours_____	horario de invierno	*ohrahryoh deh eenbyehrnoh*

1 .4 One, two, three...

0	_____	cero	*thehroh*
1	_____	uno	*oonoh*
2	_____	dos	*dohs*
3	_____	tres	*trehs*
4	_____	cuatro	*kwahtroh*

5 _____	cinco	*theenkoh*
6 _____	seis	*sehees*
7 _____	siete	*syehteh*
8 _____	ocho	*ohchoh*
9 _____	nueve	*nwehbeh*
10 _____	diez	*dyeth*
11 _____	once	*ohntheh*
12 _____	doce	*dohtheh*
13 _____	trece	*trehtheh*
14 _____	catorce	*kahtohrtheh*
15 _____	quince	*keentheh*
16 _____	dieciséis	*dyetheesehees*
17 _____	diecisiete	*dyetheesyehteh*
18 _____	dieciocho	*dyetheeohchoh*
19 _____	diecinueve	*dyetheenwehbe*
20 _____	veinte	*beheenteh*
21 _____	veintiuno	*beheenteeoonoh*
22 _____	veintidós	*beheenteheedohs*
30 _____	treinta	*treheentah*
31 _____	treinta y uno	*treheentah ee oonoh*
32 _____	treinta y dos	*treheentah ee dohs*
40 _____	cuarenta	*kwahrehntah*
50 _____	cincuenta	*theenkwehntah*
60 _____	sesenta	*sehsehntah*
70 _____	setenta	*sehtehntah*
80 _____	ochenta	*ohchehntah*
90 _____	noventa	*nohvehntah*
100 _____	cien	*thyehn*
101 _____	ciento uno	*thyehntoh oonoh*
110 _____	ciento diez	*thyehntoh dyeth*
120 _____	ciento veinte	*thyehntoh beheenteh*
200 _____	doscientos	*dohsthyehntohs*
300 _____	trescientos	*trehsthyehntohs*
400 _____	cuatrocientos	*kwahtrohthyehntohs*
500 _____	quinientos	*keenyehntohs*
600 _____	seiscientos	*seheesthyehntohs*
700 _____	setecientos	*sehtehthyehntohs*
800 _____	ochocientos	*ohchohthyehntohs*
900 _____	novecientos	*nohbehthyentohs*
1000 _____	mil	*meel*
1100 _____	mil cien	*meel thyehn*
2000 _____	dos mil	*dohs meel*
10,000 _____	diez mil	*dyeth meel*
100,000 _____	cien mil	*thyehn meel*
1,000,000 _____	un millón	*oon meelyohn*
1st _____	primero	*preemehroh*
2nd _____	segundo	*sehgoondoh*
3rd _____	tercero	*tehrthehroh*
4th _____	cuarto	*kwahrtoh*
5th _____	quinto	*keentoh*
6th _____	sexto	*sehxtoh*
7th _____	séptimo	*sehpteemoh*
8th _____	octavo	*ohktahboh*

9th _____	noveno	*nohvehnoh*
10th _____	décimo	*dehtheemoh*
11th _____	undécimo	*oondehtheemoh*
12th _____	duodécimo	*doo-ohdehtheemo*
13th _____	decimotercero	*dehtheemohtehrthehroh*
14th _____	decimocuarto	*dehtheemohkwahrtoh*
15th _____	decimoquinto	*dehtheemohkeentoh*
16th _____	decimosexto	*dehtheemohsehxtoh*
17th _____	decimoséptimo	*dehtheemosehpteemoh*
18th _____	decimoctavo	*dehtheemohktahboh*
19th _____	decimonoveno	*dehtheemonobenoh*
20th _____	vigésimo	*beeheseemoh*
21st _____	vigesimoprimero	*beeheseemohpreemeroh*
22nd _____	vigesimosegundo	*beeheseemohsegoondoh*
30th _____	trigésimo	*treeheseemoh*
100th _____	centésimo	*thentehseemoh*
1,000th _____	milésimo	*meelehseemoh*

once _____	una vez	*oonah behth*
twice _____	dos veces	*dos behthes*
double _____	el doble	*ehl dohbleh*
triple _____	el triple	*ehl treepleh*
half _____	la mitad	*lah meetath*
a quarter _____	un cuarto	*oon kwartoh*
a third _____	un tercio	*oon terthyoh*
a couple, a few, some _____	unos, algunos	*oonohs, algoonohs*

2 + 4 = 6 _____	dos más cuatro, seis	*dohs mahs kwahtroh, sehees*
4 – 2 = 2 _____	cuatro menos dos, dos	*kwahtroh mehnohs dohs, dohs*
2 x 4 = 8 _____	dos por cuatro, ocho	*dohs pohr kwahtroh, ohchoh*
4 ÷ 2 = 2 _____	cuatro dividido dos, dos	*kwahtroh deebeedeedoh dohs, dohs*

odd/even _____	par/impar	*pahr/eempahr*
total _____	(en) total	*(ehn) tohtahl*
6 x 9 _____	seis por nueve	*sehees pohr nwehbeh*

.5 The weather

Is the weather going to be good/bad?	¿Hará buen/mal tiempo?	*ahrah bwehn/mahl tyehmpoh?*
Is it going to get colder/hotter?	¿Hará más frío/calor?	*ahrah mahs freeoh/kahlohr?*

What temperature is it going to be?	¿Cuántos grados hará?
	kwahntohs grahdohs ahrah?
Is it going to rain?	¿Va a llover?
	bah ah lyohbehr?
Is there going to be a storm?	¿Tendremos tormenta?
	tehndrehmohs tohrmehntah?
Is it going to snow?	¿Va a nevar?
	bah ah nehbahr?
Is it going to freeze?	¿Va a helar?
	bah ah ehlahr?
Is the thaw setting in?	¿Comenzará el deshielo?
	kohmehnzahrah ehl dehsyeloh
Is it going to be foggy?	¿Habrá niebla?
	ahbrah nyehblah?
Is there going to be a thunderstorm?	¿Habrá tormenta eléctrica?
	ahbrah tohrmehntah ehlehktreekah?
The weather's changing	Va a cambiar el tiempo
	bah ah kahmbyahr ehl tyehmpoh
It's cooling down	Va a refrescar
	bah ah rehfrehskahr
What's the weather going to be like today/tomorrow?	¿Qué tiempo hará hoy/mañana?
	keh tyehmpoh ahrah oy/mahnyahnah?

algo	granizo	ola de calor
nublado/nublado	hail	heat wave
light/heavy clouds	...grados(bajo/sobre	pesado
bochornoso	cero)	muggy
stormy	...degrees(above/	sofocante
bueno	below zero)	scorching hot
fine	helada	soleado
caluroso	(black) ice	sunny
hot	húmedo	suave
chubasco	damp	mild
shower	huracán	tormenta eléctrica
cielo cubierto	hurricane	thunderstorm
overcast	llovizna	vendaval
desapacible	drizzle	gale
bleak	lluvia	ventoso
despejado	rain	windy
clear	lluvioso	viento
escarcha	wet	wind
frost	niebla	viento leve
fresco	fog	/moderado/ fuerte
chilly	nieve	light/moderate/
frìo	snow	strong wind
cold	nublado	tempestad
	cloudy	squall

Useful lists

1.6 Here, there...

See also 5.1 Asking for directions

here/there _____	aquí/allá
	ahkee/ahlyah
somewhere/nowhere _____	en alguna/ninguna parte
	ehn algoonah/neengoonah pahrteh
everywhere _____	en todas partes
	ehn tohdahs pahrtehs
far away/nearby _____	lejos/cerca
	lehhos/thehrkah
right/left _____	a la derecha/izquierda
	ah lah dehrehchah/eethkyehrdah
to the right/left of _____	a la derecha/izquierda de
	ah lah dehrehchah/eethkyehrdah deh
straight ahead _____	todo recto
	tohdoh rehktoh
via _____	pasando por
	pahsahndoh pohr
in _____	en
	ehn
on_____	sobre
	sohbreh
under _____	debajo de
	dehbahhoh deh
against _____	contra
	kohntrah
opposite _____	frente a
	frehnteh ah
next to _____	al lado de
	ahl lahdoh deh
near_____	junto a
	hoontoh ah
in front of_____	delante de
	dehlahnteh deh
in the centre _____	en el medio
	ehn ehl mehdyoh
forward_____	hacia adelante
	ahthyah ahdehlanteh
down_____	(hacia) abajo
	(ahthyah) ahbahhoh
up_____	(hacia) arriba
	(ahthya) ahrreebah
inside _____	(hacia) adentro
	(ahthya) ahdehntroh
outside _____	(hacia) afuera
	(ahthya) ahfwehrah
behind _____	(hacia) atrás
	(ahthya) ahtrahs
at the front _____	delante
	dehlahnteh
at the back_____	detrás
	dehtrahs
in the north _____	en el norte
	ehn ehl nohrteh

to the south _____	hacia el sur	
	ahthya ehl soor	
from the west _____	del oeste	
	dehl ohehsteh	
from the east _____	del este	
	dehl ehsteh	
...of _____	al...de	
	ahl...deh	

.7 What does that sign say?

See 5.4 Traffic signs

abierto/cerrado	horario (de apertura)	prohibido pisar el
open/closed	opening hours	césped
agua no potable	información	keep off the grass
no drinking water	information	razón aquí
alta tensión	liquidación (por	inquiries
high voltage	cese)	rebajas
ascensor	closing-down sale	clearance
lift	no funciona	recepción
caballeros	out of order	reception
gents/gentlemen	no tocar	recién pintado
caja	please do not touch	wet paint
pay here	peligro	reservado
completo	danger	reserved
full	peligro de incendio	saldos
coto privado	fire hazard	sale
private (property)	...piso	salida
cuidado con el perro	...floor	exit
beware of the dog	primeros auxilios	salida de
cuidado, escalón	first aid	emergencia/salida
mind the step	prohibido el paso	de socorro
entrada	no entry	emergency exit
entrance	prohibido fotografiar	se alquila
entrada libre	no photographs	for hire
free admission	prohibido fumar	se ruega no molestar
escalera	no smoking	do not disturb
stairs	prohibido hacer	se vende
escalera de	fuego	for sale
incendios	no open fires	señoras
fire escape	prohibido para	ladies
escalera mecánica	animales	servicios
escalator	no pets allowed	toilets
freno de emergencia		empujar/tirar
emergency brake		push/pull

.8 Telephone alphabet

a	_____ *ah*	de Antonio	*deh ahntohnyoh*
b	_____ *beh*	de Barcelona	*deh bahr-thehlohnah*
c	_____ *theh*	de Carmen	*deh kahrmehn*
ch	_____ *cheh*	de chocolate	*deh chohkohlahteh*
d	_____ *deh*	de Dolores	*deh dohlohrehs*

e	_____	eh	de Enrique	deh ehnreekeh
f	_____	hefeh	de Francia	deh frahnthyah
g	_____	heh	de Gerona	de hehrohnah
h	_____	ahcheh	de historia	de eestohryah
I	_____	ee	de Inés	deh eenehs
j	_____	hohtah	de José	deh hohseh
k	_____	kah	de Kilo	deh keeloh
l	_____	ehleh	de Lorenzo	deh lohrehnthoh
ll	_____	ehlyeh	de Llobregat	deh lyohbrehgaht
m	_____	ehmeh	de Madrid	deh Mahdreedh
n	_____	ehneh	de Navarra	deh nahbahrrah
ñ	_____	ehnyeh	de ñoño	deh nyohnyoh
o	_____	oh	de Oviedo	deh ohbyedoh
p	_____	peh	de París	deh pahrees
q	_____	koo	de querido	deh kehreedoh
r	_____	ehrreh	de Ramón	deh rahmohn
s	_____	ehseh	de sábado	deh sahbahdoh
t	_____	teh	de Tarragona	deh tahrrahgohnah
u	_____	oo	de Ulises	deh ooleesehs
v	_____	oobeh	de Valencia	deh bahlehnthyah
w	_____	oobehdohbleh	de Washington	deh wahsheengtohn
x	_____	ehkees	de Xiquena	deh heekehnah
y	_____	eegryehgah	griega	
z	_____	thehtah	de Zaragoza	deh thahrahgohthah

1.9 **P**ersonal details

surname	_____	apellidos
		ahpehlyeedohs
christian name(s)	_____	nombre
		nohmbreh
initials	_____	iniciales
		eeneethyahlehs
address (street/number)	___	dirección (calle/número)
		deerehkthyohn (kahlyeh/noomehroh)
post code/town	_____	código postal/población
		cohdeegoh pohstahl/pohblahthyon
sex (male/female)	_____	sexo (v = varón, m = mujer)
		sehksoh (v = bahrohn, m = moohehr)
nationality	_____	nacionalidad
		nahthyohnahleedahd
date of birth	_____	fecha de nacimiento
		fehchah deh nahtheemyehntoh
place of birth	_____	lugar de nacimiento
		loogahr deh natheemyehntoh
occupation	_____	profesión
		profehsyohn
married/single/divorced	___	casado, casada/soltero, soltera/
		divorciado, divorciada
		kahsahdoh, kahsahdah/sohltehroh,
		sohltehrah/deebohrthyahdoh,
		deebohrthyahdah
widowed	_____	viuda/viudo
		byoodah/byoodoh
(number of) children	_____	(número de) hijos
		(noomehroh deh) eehohs

passport/identity card/driving licence/ number, place and date of issue — pasaporte/carnet de identidad/permiso de conducir/número, lugar y fecha de expedición

kahrneh deh eedehnteedahdh (pahsahpohrteh/pehrmeesoh delı kohndootheer) noomehroh, loogahr ee fehchah deh ehkspehdeethyohn

Courtesies

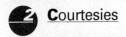 **Courtesies**

● **Female friends and relatives** kiss on both cheeks in Spain.
In shops, etc., you will hear *¡Buenos días!* or just *¡Buenas!*, and expect
to be addressed in Basque or Catalan in these provinces. For example
you will hear *¡Agur!* instead of *¡Adiós!* in the Basque Country.

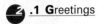
.1 Greetings

Hello, Mr Smith _____ Hola, buenos días
ohlah, bwehnohs deeahs

Hello, Peter _____ Hola, Pedro
ohlah, pehdroh

Hi, Helen _____ Qué hay, Elena
keh ay, ehlehnah

Good morning, madam_____ Buenos días, señora (before 2pm)
bwehnohs deeahs, sehnyohrah

Good afternoon, sir _____ Buenas tardes, señor (after 2pm)
bwehnahs tahrdehs, sehnyohr

Good evening_____ Buenas tardes (before 9pm), buenas
noches (after 9pm)
bwehnahs tahrdehs, bwehnahs nohchehs

How are you? _____ ¿Qué tal?
keh tahl?

Fine, thank you, and you?__ Muy bien, ¿y usted?
mwee byehn, ee oostehdh?

Very well _____ Estupendo
ehstoopehndoh

Not very well _____ Regular
rehgoolahr

Not too bad_____ Tirando
teerando

I'd better be going_____ Bueno, me voy
bwehnoh, meh boy

I have to be going. _____ Tengo que irme. Me están esperando
  Someone's waiting *tehngoh keh eermeh, meh ehstahn*
  for me *ehspehrahndoh*

Bye!_____ ¡Adiós!
ahdyohs!

Goodbye _____ Hasta luego
ahstah lwehgoh

See you soon _____ Hasta pronto
ahstah prohntoh

See you later _____ Hasta luego
ahstah lwehgoh

See you in a little while____ Hasta ahora
ahstah ahohrah

Sleep well _____ Que descanse
keh dehskahnseh

Good night _____ Buenas noches
bwehnahs nohchehs

All the best _____ Que le vaya bien
keh leh bahyah byehn

Have fun_____ Que se divierta, que lo pase bien
keh seh deebyehrtah, keh loh pahseh byehn

Good luck _____	Mucha suerte
	moochah swehrteh
Have a nice holiday _____	Felices vacaciones
	fehleethehs bahkahthyohnehs
Have a good trip _____	Buen viaje
	bwehn byah<u>h</u>eh
Thank you, you too_____	Gracias, igualmente
	grahthyahs, eegwahlmehnteh
Say hello to...for me_____	Recuerdos a...
	rehkwehrdohs ah...

.2 How to ask a question

Who?_____	¿Quién?
	kyehn?
Who's that? _____	¿Quién es?
	kyehn ehs?
What? _____	¿Qué?
	keh?
What's there to_____ see here?	¿Qué se puede visitar aquí? *keh seh pwehdeh beeseetahr ahkee?*
What kind of hotel_____ is that?	¿Qué clase de hotel es? *keh klahseh deh ohtehl ehs?*
Where? _____	¿Dónde?
	dohndeh?
Where's the toilet? _____	¿Dónde están los servicios?
	dohndeh ehstahn lohs sehrbeethyohs?
Where are you going? _____	¿A dónde va?
	ahdohndeh bah?
Where are you from? _____	¿De dónde es usted?
	deh dohndeh ehs oostehd?
How?_____	¿Cómo?
	kohmoh?
How far is that? _____	¿A qué distancia queda?
	ah keh deestahnthyah kehdah?
How long does it take? ____	¿Cuánto dura?
	kwahntoh doorah?
How long is the trip? _____	¿Cuánto dura el viaje?
	kwahntoh doorah ehl byah<u>h</u>eh?
How much?_____	¿Cuánto?
	kwahntoh?
How much is this?_____	¿Cuánto vale?
	kwahntoh bahleh?
What time is it? _____	¿Qué hora es?
	keh ohrah ehs?
Which? _____	¿Cuál? ¿Cuáles?
	kwahl? kwahlehs?
Which glass is mine? _____	¿Cuál es mi copa?
	kwahl ehs mee kohpah?
When? _____	¿Cuándo?
	kwahndoh?
When are you leaving? ____	¿Cuándo sale?
	kwahndoh sahleh?
Why?_____	¿Por qué?
	pohr keh?
Could you...me?_____	¿Podría...?
	pohdreeah...?

English	Spanish / pronunciation
Could you help me, _____ please?	¿Podría ayudarme? *pohdreeah ahyoodahrmeh?*
Could you point that_____ out to me?	¿Me lo podría indicar? *meh loh pohdreeah eendeekahr?*
Could you come _____ with me, please?	¿Le importaría acompañarme? *leh eempohrtahreeah ahkohmpahnyahrmeh?*
Could you..._____	¿Quiere...?/¿Podría...? *kyehreh...?/pohdreeah...?*
Could you reserve some ___ tickets for me, please?	¿Me podría reservar entradas? *meh pohdreeah rehsehrbahr ehntrahdahs?*
Do you know...? _____	¿Sabe...? *sahbeh...?*
Do you know another_____ hotel, please?	¿Sabría indicarme otro hotel? *sahbreeah eendeekahrmeh ohtroh ohtehl?*
Do you know whether...?___	¿Tiene...? *tyehneh...?*
Do you have a...?_____	¿Me podría dar un(a)...? *meh pohdreeah dahr oon(ah)...?*
Do you have a _____ vegetarian dish, please?	¿Tendría un plato sin carne? *tehndreeah oon plahtoh seen kahrneh?*
I'd like... _____	Quisiera... *keesyehrah...*
I'd like a kilo of apples, ___ please.	Quisiera un kilo de manzanas *keesyehrah oon keeloh deh mahnthahnahs*
Can I...?_____	¿Puedo...?/¿Se puede...? *pwehdoh...?/seh pwehdeh?*
Can I take this?_____	¿Podría llevármelo? *pohdreeah lyehbahrmehloh?*
Can I smoke here?_____	¿Se puede fumar aquí? *seh pwehdeh foomahr ahkee?*
Could I ask you _____ something?	¿Puedo hacerle una pregunta? *pwehdoh ahthehrleh oonah prehgoontah?*

2 .3 How to reply

English	Spanish / pronunciation
Yes, of course_____	Sí, claro *see, klahroh*
No, I'm sorry_____	No, lo siento *noh, loh syehntoh*
Yes, what can I do _____ for you?	Sí. ¿En qué puedo servirle? *see, ehn keh pwehdoh sehrbeerleh?*
Just a moment, please ___	Un momento, por favor *oon mohmehntoh, pohr fahbohr*
No, I don't have _____ time now	No, ahora no tengo tiempo *noh, aohrah noh tehngoh tyehmpoh*
No, that's impossible _____	No, eso es imposible *noh, ehsoh ehs eempohseebleh*
I think so _____	Creo que sí *krehoh keh see*
I agree_____	Yo también lo creo *yoh tahmbyehn loh krehoh*
I hope so too_____	Yo también lo espero *yoh tahmbyehn loh ehspehroh*
No, not at all_____	No, de ninguna manera *noh, deh neengoonah mahnehrah*
No, no-one _____	No, nadie *noh, nahdyeh*

No, nothing _____	No, nada
	noh, nahdah
That's (not) right _____	(No) es cierto
	(noh) ehs thyehrtoh
I (don't) agree _____	(No) estoy de acuerdo con usted
	(noh) ehstoy deh ahkwehrdoh kohn
	oostehdh
All right _____	Está bien
	ehstah byehn
Okay _____	Vale
	bahleh
Perhaps _____	Quizá
	keethah
I don't know _____	No lo sé
	noh loh seh

⭐ .4 Thank you

Thank you _____	Gracias
	grahthyahs
You're welcome _____	De nada
	deh nahdah
Thank you very much _____	Muchísimas gracias
	moocheeseemahs grahthyahs
Very kind of you_____	Muy amable (de su parte)
	mwee ahmahbleh (deh soo pahrteh)
I enjoyed it very much _____	Ha sido un verdadero placer
	ah seedoh oon behrdahdehroh plahthehr
Thank you for your _____	Gracias por la molestia
trouble	*grahthyahs pohr lah mohlehstyah*
You shouldn't have _____	No se hubiera molestado
	noh seh oobyehrah mohlehstahdoh
That's all right _____	No se preocupe
	noh seh prehohkoopeh

⭐ .5 Sorry

Excuse me_____	Perdone
	pehrdohneh
Sorry! _____	¡Perdone!
	pehrdohneh!
I'm sorry, I didn't know...___	Perdone, no sabía que...
	pehrdohneh, noh sahbeeah keh...
I do apologise_____	Perdone
	pehrdohneh
I'm sorry_____	Lo siento
	loh syehntoh
I didn't do it on purpose,___	No ha sido a propósito; ha sido sin querer
it was an accident	*noh ah seedoh ah prohpohseetoh; ah*
	seedoh seen kehrehr
That's all right _____	No importa
	noh eempohrtah
Never mind_____	Déjelo
	deh_hehloh
It could've happened to____	Le puede pasar a cualquiera
anyone	*leh pwehdeh pahsahr ah kwahlkyehrah*

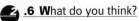

2.6 What do you think?

Which do you prefer?_____	¿Qué prefiere? *keh prehfyehreh?*
What do you think?_____	¿Qué te parece? *keh teh pahrehtheh?*
Don't you like dancing?____	¿No te gusta bailar? *noh teh goostah bahylahr?*
I don't mind_____	Me da igual *meh dah eegwahl*
Well done!_____	¡Muy bien! *mwee byehn!*
Not bad!_____	¡No está mal! *noh ehstah mahl!*
Great!_____	¡Excelente! *ehxthehlehnteh!*
Wonderful!_____	¡Qué delicia! *keh dehleethyah!*
It's really nice here!_____	¡Qué bien se está aquí! *keh byehn seh ehstah ahkee!*
How nice!_____	¡Qué mono/bonito! *keh mohnoh/bohneetoh!*
How nice for you!_____	¡Cuánto me alegro por usted! *kwahntoh meh ahlehgroh pohr oostehd!*
I'm (not) very happy_____ with...	(No) estoy muy contento con... *(noh) ehstoy mwee kohntehntoh kohn...*
I'm glad..._____	Me alegro de que... *meh ahlehgroh deh keh...*
I'm having a great time ____	Me lo estoy pasando muy bien *meh loh ehstoy pahsahndoh mwee byehn*
I'm looking forward to it __	Me hace ilusión *meh ahtheh eeloosyohn*
I hope it'll work out_____	Espero que salga bien *ehspehroh keh sahlgah byehn*
That's ridiculous!_____	¡Qué ridículo! *keh reedeekooloh!*
That's terrible!_____	¡Qué horrible! *keh ohrreebleh!*
What a pity!_____	¡Qué lástima! *keh lahsteemah!*
That's filthy!_____	¡Qué asco! *keh ahskoh!*
What a load of rubbish! ___	¡Qué tontería! *keh tohntehreeah!*
I don't like..._____	No me gusta... *noh meh goostah...*
I'm bored to death _____	Me aburro como una ostra *meh ahboorroh kohmoh oonah ohstrah*
I've had enough_____	Estoy harto(a) *ehstoy ahrtoh(ah)*
This is no good _____	No puede ser *noh pwehdeh sehr*
I was expecting _____ something completely different	Yo me había esperado otra cosa *yoh meh ahbeeah ehspehrahdoh ohtrah kohsah*

Conversation

Conversation

3.1 I beg your pardon?

I don't speak any/ I speak a little...	No hablo/hablo un poco de... *noh ahbloh/ahbloh oon pohkoh deh...*
I'm English	Soy inglés/inglesa *soy eenglehs/eenglehsah*
I'm Scottish	Soy escocés/escocesa *soy ehskohthehs/ehskothehsah*
I'm Irish	Soy irlandés/irlandesa *soy eerlahndehs/eerlahndehsah*
I'm Welsh	soy galés/galesa *soy gahlehs/gahlehsah*
Do you speak English/French/German?	¿Habla inglés/francés/alemán? *ahblah eenglehs/frahnthehs/ahlehmahn?*
Is there anyone who speaks...?	¿Hay alguien que hable...? *ay ahlgyehn ahkee keh ahbleh...?*
I beg your pardon?	¿Cómo dice? *kohmoh deetheh?*
I (don't) understand	(No) comprendo *(noh) kohmprehndoh*
Do you understand me?	¿Me entiende? *meh ehntyehndeh?*
Could you repeat that, please?	¿Le importa repetirlo? *leh eempohrtah rehpehteerloh?*
Could you speak more slowly, please?	¿Podría hablar más despacio? *pohdreeah ahblahr mahs dehspahthyo?*
What does that (word) mean?	¿Qué significa esto/esta palabra? *keh seegneefeekah ehstoh/ehstah pahlahbrah?*
Is that similar to/the same as...?	¿Es (más o menos) lo mismo que...? *ehs mahs oh mehnohs loh meesmoh keh...?*
Could you write that down for me, please?	¿Podría escribírmelo? *pohdreeah eskreebeermehloh?*
Could you spell that for me, please? (See 1.8 Telephone alphabet)	¿Podría deletreármelo? *pohdreeah dehlehtrehahrmehloh?*
Could you point that out in this phrase book, please?	¿Me lo podría señalar en esta guía? *meh loh pohdreeah sehnyahlahr ehn ehstah gheeah?*
One moment, please, I have to look it up	Espere que lo busco en la guía *ehspehreh keh loh booskoh ehn lah gheeah*
I can't find the word/the sentence	No puedo encontrar la palabra/la frase *noh pwehdoh ehnkohntrahr lah pahlahbrah/lah frahseh*
How do you say that in...?	¿Cómo se dice eso en...? *kohmoh seh deetheh ehstoh ehn...?*
How do you pronounce that?	¿Cómo se pronuncia? *kohmoh seh prohnoonthyah?*

3

Conversation

May I introduce myself? ___	Permítame presentarme
	pehrmeetahmeh prehsehntahrmeh
My name's... ___	Me llamo...
	meh lyahmoh...
I'm... ___	Soy...
	soy...
What's your name? ___	¿Cómo se llama?
	kohmoh seh lyahmah?
May I introduce...? ___	Permítame presentarle a...
	pehrmeetahmeh prehsehntahrleh ah...
This is my wife/ ___ daughter/mother/ girlfriend	Esta es mi mujer/mi hija/mi madre/mi amiga
	ehstah ehs mee moohehr/mee eehah /mee mahdreh/mee ahmeegah
– my husband/son/ ___ father/boyfriend.	Este es mi marido/mi hijo/mi padre/mi amigo
	ehsteh ehs mee mahreedoh/mee eehoh/mee pahdreh/mee ahmeegoh
How do you do ___	Hola, mucho gusto
	ohlah, moochoh goostoh
Pleased to meet you ___	Encantado(a) (de conocerle)
	ehnkahntahdoh(ah) (deh kohnohthehrleh)
Where are you from? ___	¿De dónde es usted?
	deh dohndeh ehs oostehdh?
I'm from ___ England/Scotland/ Ireland/Wales	Soy inglés/esa escocés/esa irlandés/esa galés/esa
	soy eenglehs/ehsah ehskohthehs/ehsah eerlahndehs/ehsah gahlehs/ ehsah
What city do you live in? ___	¿En qué ciudad vive?
	ehn keh thyoodahdh beebeh?
In..., It's near... ___	En...Eso está cerca de...
	ehn...ehsoh ehstah thehrkah deh...
Have you been here ___ long?	¿Hace mucho que está aquí?
	ahtheh moochoh keh ehstah ahkee?
A few days ___	Unos días
	oonohs deeahs
How long are you ___ staying here?	¿Cuánto tiempo piensa quedarse?
	kwahntoh tyehmpoh pyehnsah kehdahrseh?
We're (probably) ___ leaving tomorrow/ in two weeks	Nos iremos (probablemente) mañana/dentro de dos semanas
	nohs eerehmohs (prohbahblehmehnteh) mahnyahnah/dehntroh deh dohs sehmahnahs
Where are you staying? ___	¿Dónde se aloja?
	dohndeh seh ahlohhah?
In a hotel/an apartment ___	En un hotel/apartamento
	ehn oon ohtehl/ahpahrtahmehntoh
On a camp site ___	En un camping
	ehn oon kahmpeen
With friends/relatives ___	En casa de amigos/parientes
	ehn kahsah deh ahmeegohs/pahryehntehs
Are you here on your ___ own/with your family?	¿Ha venido solo(a)/con su familia?
	ah behneedoh sohloh(ah)/kohn soo fahmeelyah?

I'm on my own	He venido solo(a)
	eh behneedoh sohloh(ah)
I'm with my partner/wife/husband	con mi pareja/mujer/marido
	kohn mee pahrehhah/moohehr/mahreedoh
– with my family	con mi familia
	kohn mee fahmeelyah
– with relatives	con unos parientes
	kohn oonohs pahryehntehs
– with a friend/friends	con un amigo/una amiga/unos amigos
	kohn oon ahmeegoh/oonah ahmeegah/oonohs ahmeegohs
Are you married?	¿Está casado/casada?
	ehstah kahsahdoh/kahsahdah?
Do you have a steady boyfriend/girlfriend?	¿Tienes novio/novia?
	tyehnehs nohbyoh/nohbyah?
That's none of your business.	No es asunto suyo
	noh ehs ahsoontoh sooyoh
I'm married	Soy casado
	soy kahsahdoh
– single	Soy soltero
	soy sohltehroh
– separated	Estoy separado
	ehstoy sehpahrahdoh
– divorced	Estoy divorciado
	ehstoy deebohrthyahdoh
– a widow/widower	Soy viuda/viudo
	soy byoodah/byoodoh
I live alone/with someone	Vivo solo(a)/con otra persona
	beeboh sohloh(ah)/kohn ohtrah pehrsohnah
Do you have any children/grandchildren?	¿Tiene hijos/nietos?
	tyehneh eehohs/nyehtohs?
How old are you?	¿Cuántos años tiene?
	kwahntohs ahnyohs tyehneh?
How old is she/he?	¿Cuántos años tiene?
	kwahntohs ahnyohs tyehneh?
I'm...	Tengo...años
	tehngoh...ahnyohs
She's/he's...	Tiene...años
	tyehneh...ahnyohs
What do you do for a living?	¿En qué trabaja?
	ehn keh trahbahhah?
I work in an office	Trabajo en una oficina
	trahbahhoh ehn oonah ohfeetheenah
I'm a student/ I'm at school	Estudio
	ehstoodyoh
I'm unemployed	Estoy en paro
	ehstoy ehn pahroh
I'm retired	Soy jubilado
	soy hoobeelahdoh
I'm on a disability pension	Tengo una pensión de invalidez
	tehngoh oonah pehnsyohn deh eenbahleedeth
I'm a housewife	Soy ama de casa
	soy ahmah deh kahsah
Do you like your job?	¿Le gusta su trabajo?
	leh goostah soo trahbahhoh?

Most of the time _____	A veces sí, a veces no
	ah behthehs see, ah behthehs noh
I usually do, but I prefer ___ holidays	Por lo general sí, pero prefiero las vacaciones
	pohr loh <u>h</u>ehnehrahl see, pehroh prehfyehroh lahs bahkahthyohnehs

3.3 Starting/ending a conversation

Could I ask you _____ something?	¿Podría preguntarle una cosa?
	pohdreeah prehgoontahrleh oonah kohsah?
Excuse me	Perdone
	pehrdohneh
Excuse me, could you ____ help me?	¿Podría ayudarme?
	pohdreeah ahyoodahrmeh?
Yes, what's the problem? __	Sí, ¿qué pasa?
	see, keh pahsah?
What can I do for you? ____	¿En qué puedo servirle?
	ehn keh pwehdoh sehrbeerleh?
Sorry, I don't have time ____ now	Lo siento, ahora no tengo tiempo
	loh syehntoh, ahohrah noh tehngoh tyehmpoh
Do you have a light? _____	¿Tiene fuego?
	tyehneh fwehgoh?
May I join you? _____	¿Le importa que me siente?
	leh eempohrtah keh meh syehnteh?
Could you take a _____ picture of me/us? Press this button.	¿Podría sacarme/sacarnos una foto? Hay que apretar este botón
	pohdreeah sahkahrmeh/sahkahrnohs oonah fohtoh? ay keh ahprehtahr ehsteh bohtohn
Leave me alone _____	Déjeme en paz
	deh<u>h</u>ehmeh ehn pahth
Get lost_____	Váyase al diablo
	bahyahseh ahl deeahbloh
Go away or I'll scream____	Como no se vaya, grito
	kohmoh noh seh bahyah, greetoh

3.4 Congratulations and condolences

Happy birthday/many_____ happy returns	Feliz cumpleaños/felicidades
	fehleeth koomplehahnyohs/fehleetheedahdehs
Please accept my_____ condolences.	Le acompaño en el sentimiento
	leh ahkohmpahnyoh ehn ehl sehnteemyehntoh
I'm very sorry for you ____	¡Cuánto lo siento por usted!
	kwahntoh loh syehntoh pohr oostehdh!

3.5 A chat about the weather

See also 1.5 The weather

It's so hot/cold today!_____	¡Qué calor/frío hace hoy!
	keh kahlohr/freeoh ahtheh oy!
Nice weather, isn't it? _____	¡Qué buen tiempo hace! ¿Verdad?
	keh bwehn tyehmpoh ahtheh! behrdah?

What a wind/storm! __ ____	¡Vaya viento/tormenta!
	bahyah byehntoh/tohrmentah!
All that rain/snow! _____	¡Cómo llueve/nieva!
	kohmoh lywehbeh/nyehbah!
All that fog! _____	¡Cuánta niebla!
	kwahntah nyehblah!
Has the weather been ____	¿Hace mucho que hace este tiempo?
like this for long here?	*ahtheh moochoh keh ahtheh ehsteh*
	tyehmpoh?
Is it always this hot/cold ___	¿Aquí siempre hace tanto calor/frío?
here?	*ahkee syehmpreh ahtheh tahntoh*
	kahlohr/freeoh?
Is it always this dry/wet____	¿Aquí siempre hace un tiempo tan
here?	seco/lluvioso?
	ahkee syehmpreh ahtheh oon tyehmpoh
	tahn sehkoh/lyoobyohsoh?

3.6 Hobbies

Do you have any _____	¿Tiene algún hobby?
hobbies?	*tyehneh algoon hohbee?*
I like painting/_____	Me gusta pintar/leer/la fotografía/el
reading/photography/	bricolaje
DIY	*meh goostah peentahr/lehehr/lah*
	fohtohgrahfeeah/ehl breekohlahheh
I like music _____	Me gusta la música
	meh goostah lah mooseekah
I like playing the _____	Me gusta tocar la guitarra/el piano
guitar/piano	*meh goostah tohkahr lah gueetahrrah/ehl*
	pyahnoh
I like going to the movies __	Me gusta ir al cine
	meh goostah eer ahl theeneh
I like travelling/_____	Me gusta viajar/hacer deporte/pescar/salir
sport/fishing/walking	a caminar
	meh goostah byahhahr/ahthehr
	dehpohrteh/pehskahr/sahleer
	ah kahmeenahr

3.7 Being the host(ess)

See also 4 Eating out

Can I offer you a drink? ____	¿Le gustaría algo de beber?
	leh goostahreeah ahlgoh deh
	behbehr?
What would you like_____	¿Qué quieres beber?
to drink?	*keh kyehrehs behbehr?*
Something non-alcoholic,__	Algo sin alcohol
please.	*ahlgoh seen ahlkohl*
Would you like a _____	¿Quiere un cigarrillo/un puro/liar un
cigarette/cigar/to roll	cigarrillo?
your own?	*kyehreh oon theegahrreelyoh/oon*
	poohroh/leeahr oon theegahrreelyoh?
I don't smoke _____	No fumo
	noh foomoh

Conversation

3.8 Invitations

Are you doing anything____ tonight?	¿Tiene algo que hacer esta noche? *tyehneh ahlgoh keh ahthehr ehstah nohcheh?*
Do you have any plans ____ for today/this afternoon/tonight?	¿Ya tiene planes para hoy/ esta tarde/esta noche? *yah tyehneh plahnehs pahrah oy/ehstah tahrdeh/ehstah nohcheh?*
Would you like to go _____ out with me?	¿Le(te) apetece salir conmigo? *leh(teh) ahpehtehtheh sahleer kohnmeegoh?*
Would you like to go _____ dancing with me?	¿Le(te) apetece ir a bailar conmigo? *leh(teh) ahpehtehtheh eer ah baylahr kohnmeegoh?*
Would you like to have ____ lunch/dinner with me?	¿Le(te) apetece comer/cenar conmigo? *leh(teh) ahpehtehtheh kohmehr/thenahr kohnmeegoh?*
Would you like to come____ to the beach with me?	¿Le(te) apetece ir a la playa conmigo? *leh(teh) ahpehtehtheh eer ah lah plahyah kohnmeegoh?*
Would you like to come____ into town with us?	¿Le apetece ir a la ciudad con nosotros? *leh ahpehtehtheh eer ah lah thyoodahdh kohn nohsohtrohs?*
Would you like to come____ and see some friends with us?	¿Le apetece ir a casa de unos amigos con nosotros? *leh ahpehtehtheh eer ah kahsah deh oonohs ahmeegohs kohn nohsohtrohs?*
Shall we dance?_____	¿Bailamos? *baylahmohs?*
– sit at the bar? _____	¿Vienes a sentarte conmigo en la barra? *byehnehs ah sehntahrteh kohnmeegoh ehn lah bahrrah?*
– get something to drink? __	¿Vamos a beber algo? *bahmohs ah behbehr ahlgoh?*
– go for a walk/drive?_____	¿Vamos a dar una vuelta? *bahmohs ah dahr oonah bwehltah?*
Yes, all right _____	Sí, vamos *see, bahmohs*
Good idea _____	Buena idea *bwehnah eedehah*
No (thank you) _____	No (gracias) *noh (grahthyahs)*
Maybe later_____	Quizá más tarde *keethah mahs tahrdeh*
I don't feel like it _____	No me apetece *noh meh ahpehtehtheh*
I don't have time _____	No tengo tiempo *noh tehngoh tyehmpoh*
I already have a date _____	Ya tengo otro compromiso *yah tehngoh ohtroh kohmprohmeesoh*
I'm not very good at_____ dancing/volleyball/ swimming	No sé bailar/jugar al vóleibol/nadar *noh seh baylahr/_h_oogahr ahl vohleheebohl/nahdahr*

3.9 Paying a compliment

English	Spanish
You look wonderful! _____	¡Qué guapo/guapa está(estás)!
	keh wahpoh/wahpah ehstah(ehstahs)!
I like your car! _____	¡Qué bonito coche!
	keh bohneetoh kohcheh!
I like your ski outfit! _____	¡Qué bonito traje de esquiar!
	keh bohneetoh trahheh deh ehskeeahr!
You're a nice boy/girl _____	Eres muy bueno/buena
	ehrehs mwee bwehnoh/bwehnah
What a sweet child! _____	¡Qué niño tan majo/niña tan maja!
	keh neenyoh tahn mahhoh/neenyah tahn mahhah!
You're a wonderful _____ dancer!	Bailas muy bien
	bahylahs mwee byehn
You're a wonderful _____ cook!	Cocinas muy bien
	kohtheenahs mwee byehn
You're a terrific soccer _____ player!	Juegas muy bien al fútbol
	hwehgahs mwee byehn ahl footbohl

3.10 Chatting someone up

English	Spanish
I like being with you _____	Me gusta estar contigo
	meh goostah ehstahr kohnteegoh
I've missed you so much __	Te he echado mucho de menos
	teh eh ehchahdoh moochoh deh mehnohs
I dreamt about you _____	He soñado contigo
	eh sohnyahdoh kohnteegoh
I think about you all day ___	Pienso todo el día en ti
	pyehnsoh tohdoh ehl deeah ehn tee
You have such a sweet ____ smile	Tienes una sonrisa muy bonita
	tyehnehs oonah sohnreesah mwee bohneetah
You have such beautiful ___ eyes	Tienes unos ojos muy bonitos
	tyehnehs oonohs ohhohs mwee bohneetohs
I'm in love with you _____	Estoy enamorado/enamorada de ti
	ehstoy ehnahmohrahdoh/ehnahmohrahdah deh tee
I'm in love with you too ___	Yo también de ti
	yoh tahmbyehn deh tee
I love you_____	Te quiero
	teh kyehroh
I love you too _____	Yo también a ti
	yoh tahmbyehn ah tee
I don't feel as strongly _____ about you	Yo no siento lo mismo por ti
	yoh noh syehntoh loh meesmoh pohr tee
I already have a _____ boyfriend/girlfriend	Ya tengo pareja
	yah tehngoh pahrehhah
I'm not ready for that_____	Yo no estoy preparado(a)
	yoh noh ehstoy prehpahrahdoh/ah
This is going too fast _____ for me	Vamos demasiado rápido
	bahmohs dehmahsyahdoh rahpeedoh
Take your hands off me____	No me toque(s)
	noh meh tohkeh(s)
Okay, no problem _____	Vale, no importa
	bahleh, noh eempohrtah

Will you stay with me tonight?	¿Te quedas a dormir? *teh kehdahs ah dohrmeer?*
I'd like to go to bed with you	Me gustaría acostarme contigo *meh goostahreeah ahkohstahrmeh kohnteegoh*
Only if we use a condom	Sólo si usamos condón *sohloh see oosahmohs kohndohn*
We have to be careful about AIDS	Hay que tener cuidado por lo del Sida *ay keh tehnehr kweedahdoh pohr loh dehl seedah*
That's what they all say	Eso es lo que dicen todos *ehsoh ehs loh keh deethehn tohdohs*
We shouldn't take any risks	Más vale no arriesgarse *mahs bahleh noh ahrryehsgahrseh*
Do you have a condom?	¿Llevas condones? *lyehbahs kohndohnehs?*
No? In that case we won't do it	¿No? Pues entonces no *noh? pwehs ehntohnthehs noh*

3.11 Arrangements

When will I see you again?	¿Cuándo te veo? *kwahndoh teh behoh?*
Are you free over the weekend?	¿Tiene tiempo este fin de semana? *tyehneh tyehmpoh ehsteh feen deh sehmahnah?*
What shall we arrange?	¿Cómo quedamos? *kohmoh kehdahmohs?*
Where shall we meet?	¿Dónde nos encontramos? *dohndeh nohs ehnkohntrahmohs?*
Will you pick me/us up?	¿Me/nos pasa a buscar? *meh/nohs pahsah ah booskahr?*
Shall I pick you up?	¿Lo/la paso a buscar? *loh/lah pahsoh ah booskahr?*
I have to be home by...	Tengo que estar en casa a las... *tehngoh keh ehstahr ehn kahsah ah lahs...*
I don't want to see you anymore	No quiero volver a verlo/verla *noh kyehroh bohlbehr ah behrloh/behrlah*

3.12 Saying goodbye

Can I take you home?	¿Lo/la acompaño a su casa? *loh/lah ahkohmpahnyoh ah soo kahsah?*
Can I write/call you?	¿Puedo escribirle/llamarlo/llamarla por teléfono? *pwehdoh ehskreebeerleh /lyahmahrloh/ lyahmahrlah pohr tehlehfohnoh?*
Will you write/call me?	¿Me escribirá/llamará por teléfono? *meh ehskreebeerah/lyahmahrah pohr tehlehfohnoh?*
Can I have your address/phone number?	¿Me da su dirección/número de teléfono? *meh dah soo deerehkthyohn/noomehroh deh tehlehfohnoh?*
Thanks for everything	Gracias por todo *grahthyahs pohr tohdoh*
It was very nice	Lo hemos pasado muy bien *loh ehmohs pahsahdoh mwee byehn*

Say hello to... _____	Recuerdos a... *rehkwehrdohs ah...*
All the best _____	Te deseo lo mejor *teh dehsehoh loh meh<u>h</u>ohr*
Good luck _____	Que te vaya bien *keh teh bahyah byehn*
When will you be back? ___	¿Cuándo vuelves? *kwahndoh bwehlbehs?*
I'll be waiting for you _____	Te esperaré *teh ehspehrahreh.*
I'd like to see you again _____	Me gustaría volver a verte *meh goostahreeah bohlbehr ah behrteh*
I hope we meet _____ again soon	Espero que nos volvamos a ver pronto *ehspehroh keh nohs bohlbahmohs ah behr* *prohntoh*
This is our address. _____ If you're ever in the UK	Esta es nuestra dirección. Si alguna vez pasa por el Reino Unido... *ehstah ehs nwehstrah deerehkthyohn. see* *ahlgoonah behth pahsah pohr ehl reheenoh* *ooneedoh...*
You'd be more than _____ welcome	Está cordialmente invitado *ehstah kohrdyahlmehnteh eenbeetahdoh*

Eating out

4 Eating out

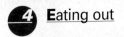

● **In Spain** people usually have three meals:

1 *El desayuno* (breakfast) approximately between 7 and 10 am.
Breakfast is light and consists of *café con leche* (white coffee), a
croissant or *suizo* (light sugary bun) or *tostadas* (toast).

2 *El almuerzo* (lunch) approx. between 2 and 4 pm, though hotels
usually serve at standard times. Lunch always includes a hot dish and
is the most important meal of the day. Office workers and
schoolchildren still lunch at home. It usually consists of four courses:
– starter (which can be a plate of greens)
– main course
– dessert
– fruit

3 *La cena* (dinner) between 9 and 11pm, 8pm in most hotels. Dinner is
usually a light, hot meal, taken with the family.

At around 6 or 7pm, a snack (*la merienda*) is often served, consisting
frequently of sandwiches with *chorizo* or *jamón serrano* and *pastas*
(biscuits) or small cakes.

Pinchos and *tapas* are often taken at bars with an apéritif, either in the
late morning or the evening.

4 .1 On arrival

I'd like to book a table for seven o'clock, please	¿Podría reservar una mesa para las siete? *pohdreeah rehsehrbahr oonah mehsah pahrah lahs syehteh?*
I'd like a table for two, please	Quisiera una mesa para dos personas *keesyehrah oonah mehsah pahrah dohs pehrsohnahs*
We've/we haven't booked	(No) hemos reservado *(noh) ehmohs rehsehrbahdoh*
Is the restaurant open yet?	¿Ya está abierto el restaurante? *yah ehstah ahbyehrtoh ehl rehstahoorahnteh?*
What time does the restaurant open/close?	¿A qué hora abre/cierra el restaurante? *ah keh ohrah ahbreh/thyehrrah ehl rehstahoorahnteh?*
Can we wait for a table?	¿Podemos esperar hasta que se desocupe una mesa? *pohdehmohs ehspehrahr ahstah keh seh dehsohkoopeh oonah mehsah?*
Do we have to wait long?	¿Tenemos que esperar mucho? *tehnehmohs keh ehspehrahr moochoh?*

¿Ha reservado mesa?	Do you have a reservation?
¿A nombre de quién?	What name, please?
Por aquí, por favor.	This way, please
Esta mesa está reservada	This table is reserved
En quince minutos quedará libre una mesa	We'll have a table free in fifteen minutes.
¿Le importaría esperar (en la barra)?	Would you like to wait (at the bar)?

35

Is this seat taken? _____	¿Está ocupada esta silla?
	ehstah ohkoopahdah ehstah seelyah?
Could we sit here/there? ___	¿Podemos sentarnos aquí/allí?
	pohdehmohs sehntahrnohs ahkee/ahlyee?
Can we sit by the_____ window?	¿Podemos sentarnos junto a la ventana?
	pohdehmohs sehntahrnohs hoontoh ah lah behntahnah?
Can we eat outside? _____	¿Podemos comer afuera?
	pohdehmohs kohmehr ahfwehrah?
Do you have another _____ chair for us?	¿Podría traernos otra silla?
	pohdreeah trahehrnohs ohtrah seelyah?
Do you have a _____ highchair?	¿Podría traernos una silla para niños?
	pohdreeah trahehrnohs oonah seelyah pahrah neenyohs?
Is there a socket for this bottle-warmer?	¿Hay un enchufe para este calentador de biberones?
	ay oon ehnchoofeh pahrah ehsteh kahlehntahdohr deh beebehrohnehs?
Could you warm up _____ this bottle/jar for me?	¿Podría calentarme este biberón/este bote?
	pohdreeah kahlehntahrmeh ehsteh beebehrohn/ehsteh bohteh?
Not too hot, please _____	Que no esté muy caliente, por favor
	keh noh ehsteh mwee kahlyehnteh pohr fahbohr
Is there somewhere I _____ can change the baby's nappy?	¿Hay algún lugar para cambiar al bebé?
	ay ahlgoon loogahr pahrah kahmbyahr ahl behbeh?
Where are the toilets? _____	¿Dónde están los servicios?
	* *dohnde ehstahn lohs sehrbeethyohs?*

🔴 .2 Ordering

Waiter! _____	¡Camarero!
	kahmahrehroh!
Madam!/Sir! _____	¡Oiga, (por favor)!
	oygah (pohr fahbohr)!
We'd like something to ___ eat/a drink	Quisiéramos comer/beber algo
	keesyehrahmohs kohmehr/behber ahlgoh
Could I have a quick_____ meal?	¿Podría comer algo rápido?
	pohdreeah kohmehr ahlgoh rahpeedoh?
We don't have much _____ time	Tenemos poco tiempo
	tehnehmohs pohkoh tyehmpoh
We'd like to have a _____ drink first	Antes quisiéramos beber algo
	ahntehs keesyehrahmohs behbehr ahlgoh
Could we see the_____ menu/wine list, please?	¿Nos podría traer la carta/la carta de vinos?
	nohs pohdreeah trahehr lah kahrtah/lah kahrtah deh beenohs?
Do you have a menu _____ in English?	¿Tienen menú en inglés?
	tyehnehn mehnoo ehn eenglehs?
Do you have a dish_____ of the day?	¿Tienen menú del día/menú turístico?
	tyehnehn mehnoo dehl deeah/mehnoo tooreesteekoh?
We haven't made a_____ choice yet	Todavía no hemos elegido
	tohdahbeeah noh ehmohs ehlehheedoh

What do you recommend?	¿Qué nos recomienda? *keh nohs rehkohmyehndah?*
What are the specialities of the region/the house?	¿Cuáles son las especialidades de la región/de la casa? *kwahlehs sohn lahs ehspehthyahleedahdehs deh lah reh<u>h</u>yohn/deh lah kahsah?*
I like strawberries/olives	Me gustan las fresas/las aceitunas *meh goostahn lahs frehsahs/lahs ahtheheetoonahs*
I don't like meat/fish/...	No me gusta el pescado/la carne/... *noh meh goostah ehl pehskahdoh/lah kahrneh/...*
What's this?	¿Qué es esto? *keh ehs ehstoh?*
Does it have...in it?	¿Lleva...? *lyehbah...?*
What does it taste like?	¿A qué sabe? *ah keh sahbeh?*
Is this a hot or a cold dish?	¿Es un plato caliente o frío? *ehs oon plahtoh kahlyehnteh oh freeoh?*
Is this sweet?	¿Es un plato dulce? *ehs oon plahtoh doolthe?*
Is this spicy?	¿Es un plato picante? *ehs oon plahtoh peekahnteh?*
Do you have anything else, please?	¿Tendría otra cosa? *tehndreeah ohtrah kohsah?*
I'm on a salt-free diet	No puedo comer sal *noh pwehdoh kohmehr sahl*
I can't eat pork	No puedo comer carne de cerdo *noh pwehdoh kohmehr kahrneh deh thehrdoh*
– sugar	No puedo comer azúcar *noh pwehdo kohmehr ahthookahr*
– fatty foods	No puedo comer grasa *noh pwehdoh kohmehr grahsah*
– (hot) spices	No puedo comer cosas picantes *noh pwehdoh kohmehr kohsahs peekahntehs*
I'll/we'll have what those people are having	Lo mismo que esos señores, por favor *loh meesmoh keh ehsohs sehnyohrehs pohr fahbohr*

¿Van a tomar un aperitivo?	Would you like a drink first?
¿Ya han elegido?	Have you decided?
¿Qué van a tomar?	What would you like to eat?
Que aproveche	Enjoy your meal.
¿Quiere su bistec rojo, mediano o muy hecho?	Would you like your steak rare, medium or well done?
¿Van a tomar postre/café?	Would you like a dessert/coffee?

I'd like...	Para mí...
	pahrah mee...
We're not having a _____ starter	No vamos a comer primer plato
	noh bahmohs ah kohmehr preemehr plahtoh
The child will share_____ what we're having	El niño/la niña comerá de nuestro menú
	ehl neenyoh/lah neenyah kohmehrah deh nwehstroh mehnoo
Could I have some _____ more bread, please?	Más pan, por favor
	mahs pahn pohr fahbohr
– a bottle of water/wine_____	Otra botella de agua/de vino, por favor
	ohtrah bohtehlyah deh ahgwah/deh beenoh, pohr fahbohr
– another helping of... _____	Otra ración de..., por favor
	ohtrah rahthyohn deh..., pohr fahbohr
– some salt and pepper_____	¿Podría traerme sal y pimienta?
	pohdreeah trahehrmeh sahl ee peemyehntah?
– a napkin _____	¿Podría traerme una servilleta?
	pohdreeah trahehrmeh oonah sehrbeelyehtah?
– a spoon_____	¿Podría traerme una cuchara?
	pohdreeah trahehrmeh oonah koochahrah?
– an ashtray _____	¿Podría traerme un cenicero?
	pohdreeah trahehrmeh oon thehneethehroh?
– some matches_____	¿Podría traerme unas cerillas?
	pohdreeah trahehrmeh oonahs thehreelyahs?
– some toothpicks_____	¿Podría traerme unos palillos?
	pohdreeah trahehrmeh oonohs pahleelyohs?
– a glass of water _____	¿Podría traerme un vaso de agua?
	pohdreeah trahehrmeh oon bahsoh deh ahgwah?
– a straw (for the child) _____	¿Podría traerme una pajita (para el niño/la niña)?
	pohdreeah trahehrmeh oonah pahheetah (pahrah ehl neenyoh/lah neenyah)?
Enjoy your meal!_____	¡Que aproveche!
	keh ahprohbehcheh!
You too! _____	Igualmente
	eegwahlmehnteh
Cheers!_____	¡Salud!
	sahloodh!
The next round's on me ___	La próxima ronda la pago yo
	lah prohxeemah rohndah lah pahgoh yoh
Could we have a doggy_____ bag, please?	¿Podemos llevarnos las sobras?
	pohdehmohs lyehbarnohs lahs sohbrahs?

4 .3 The bill

See also 8.2 Settling the bill

How much is this dish? _____	¿Cuánto vale este plato?
	kwahntoh bahleh ehsteh plahtoh?
Could I have the bill, _____ please?	La cuenta, por favor
	lah kwehntah, pohr fahbohr
All together _____	Todo junto
	tohdoh hoontoh

Everyone pays separately___	Cada uno paga lo suyo
	kahdah oonoh pahgah loh sooyoh
Could we have the menu ___ again, please?	¿Podría traernos otra vez la carta?
	pohdreeah trahehrnohs ohtrah behth lah kahrtah?
The...is not on the bill _____	Ha olvidado apuntar el/la...
	ah olbeedahdoh ahpoontahr ehl/lah...

🍴 .4 Complaints

It's taking a very_____ long time	Están tardando mucho
	ehstahn tahrdahndoh moochoh
We've been here an _____ hour already	Ya llevamos una hora aquí
	yah lyebahmohs oonah ohrah ahkee
This must be a mistake ___	Esto tiene que ser una equivocación
	ehstoh tyehneh keh sehr oonah ehkeebohkahthyohn
This is not what I_____ ordered	Esto no es lo que he pedido
	ehstoh noh ehs loh keh eh pehdeedoh
I ordered..._____	He pedido...
	eh pehdeedoh...
There's a dish missing_____	Falta un plato
	fahltah oon plahtoh
This is broken/not clean ___	Esto está roto/no está limpio
	ehstoh ehstah rohtoh/noh ehstah leempyoh
The food's cold _____	La comida está fría
	lah kohmeedah ehstah freeah
– not fresh _____	La comida no es fresca
	lah kohmeedah noh ehs frehskah
– too salty/sweet/spicy_____	La comida está muy salada/dulce/picante
	lah kohmeedah ehstah mwee sahlahdah/dooltheh/peekahnteh
The meat's not done_____	La carne está cruda
	lah kahrneh ehstah kroodah
– overdone _____	La carne está muy hecha
	lah kahrneh ehstah mwee ehchah
– tough _____	La carne está dura
	lah kahrneh ehstah doorah
– off_____	La carne está podrida
	lah kahrneh ehstah pohdreedah
Could I have something ___ else instead of this?	¿Me podría traer otra cosa en lugar de esto?
	meh pohdreeah trahehr ohtrah kohsah ehn loogahr deh ehstoh?
The bill/this amount is _____ not right	La cuenta/este precio está mal
	lah kwehntah/ehsteh prehthyoh ehstah mahl
We didn't have this_____	Esto no lo hemos comido/bebido
	ehstoh noh loh ehmohs kohmeedoh/behbeedoh
There's no paper in the ___ toilet	No hay papel en el servicio
	noh ay pahpehl ehn ehl sehrbeethyoh
Do you have a _____ complaints book?	¿Tienen libro de quejas?
	tyehnen leebroh deh keh<u>h</u>as?
Will you call the_____ manager, please?	Haga el favor de llamar al jefe
	ahgah ehl fahbohr deh lyamahr ahl <u>h</u>ehfeh

39

.5 Paying a compliment

That was a wonderful ____ meal	Hemos comido muy bien *ehmohs kohmeedoh mwee byehn*
The food was excellent ____	La comida ha estado exquisita *lah kohmeedah ah ehstahdoh ehxkeeseetah*
The...in particular was ____ delicious	Sobre todo nos ha gustado el/la... *sohbreh tohdoh nohs ah goostahdoh ehl/lah...*

.6 The menu

aperitivo apéritif	mariscos seafood	postres sweets/dessert
aves poultry	pastelería pastry	primeros platos starters
azúcar sugar	pescados fish	raciones portions
bebidas alcohólicas alcoholic beverages	platos calientes hot dishes	servicio incluido service included
bebidas calientes hot beverages	platos combinados combined dishes	sopas soups
carta de vinos wine list	plato del día dish of the day	tapas tapas
cócteles cocktails	platos fríos cold dishes	venado game
cubierto cover charge	platos principales main courses	verduras vegetables
entremeses variados hors d'oeuvres	platos típicos regional specialities	

.7 Alphabetical list of drinks and dishes

aceituna olive	anís aniseed	biftec steak
aguacate avocado	apio celery	bizcocho (borracho) sponge cake(with sherry or similar)
ajo garlic	arenque herring	bocadillo sandwich
albóndigas meat balls	arroz rice	buey/vaca beef
alcachofa artichoke	asado roast, roasted	cabrito kid
almejas clams	atún/bonito tuna	café (solo/con leche) coffee (black/white)
almendras almonds	avellana hazelnut	calamares (en su tinta) squid (cooked in their ink)
ancas de rana frog's legs	bacalao cod	caldo broth
anchoa/boquerón anchovy	batido de... ...milk shake	callos tripe
anguila eel	berenjena aubergine	

Spanish	English
cangrejo	crab
caracoles	snails
carne	meat
carpa	carp
castaña	chestnut
cebolla	onion
cerdo	pork
cerezas	cherries
cerveza	beer
chorizo	chorizo (paprika flavoured salami sausage)
chucrut	sauerkraut
chuleta/costilla	chop
churros	fritters
ciervo	venison
cigalas	Dublin Bay prawns
ciruela	plum
cochinillo asado	roast suckling pig
cocido	boiled
codorniz	quail
col/berza	cabbage
coles de Bruselas	Brussels sprouts
coliflor	cauliflower
coñac	brandy
conejo	rabbit
copa helada/helado	ice cream
cordero	lamb
crema/nata	cream
criadillas/mollejas	sweetbreads
crudo	raw
cuba libre	rum coke
dátil	date
dulce	sweet
emperador	swordfish
en escabeche	pickled
endibia	chicory/endive
ensalada (mixta)	mixed salad
ensaladilla rusa	Russian salad
escalope	escalope
espárragos	asparagus
especies	spices
espinaca	spinach
fideos	noodles
filete	fillet
flan	cream caramel
frambuesa	raspberry
fresa	strawberry
frito	fried
fruta (del tiempo)	seasonal fruit
galleta	biscuit
gambas	prawns
garbanzos	chick peas
gazpacho andaluz	gazpacho (cold soup)
granizado de limón/café	iced drink (lemon/coffee)
grosellas	red/black currants
guisado	stew
guisantes	peas
habas	broad beans
harina	flour
hígado de oca	goose liver
higo	fig
huevos al plato/ duros/revueltos	fried/hard boiled/scrambled eggs
jamón de York/serrano	ham (cooked/Parma style)
jerez (seco, dulce)	sherry (dry, sweet)
judías verdes	French beans
jugo/zumo	fruit juice
langosta	lobster
langostino	crayfish
leche	milk
lechuga	lettuce
legumbres	vegetables (legumes)
lengua	tongue
lenguado	sole
lentejas	lentils
licor	liqueur
liebre	hare
limón	lemon
lomo de cerdo	tenderloin of pork

maíz (mazorca)
corn (on the cob)
mantequilla
butter
manzana
apple
mazapán
marzipan
mejillones
mussels
melocotón (en
  almíbar)
peach (in syrup)
melón
melon
membrillo
quince
merluza
hake
mermelada
jam
mero
sea bass
morcilla
black pudding
mostaza
mustard
muslo de pollo
drumstick
nuez
walnut
ostras
oysters
paella
paella
pan
bread
pastel
cake
patatas fritas
chips/crisps
pato (silvestre)
(wild) duck
pechuga (de pollo)
(chicken) breast
pepino
cucumber
pepinillos
gherkins
pera
pear

perdiz
partridge
perejil
parsley
pescado
fish
picadillo de ternera
minced veal
pierna (de cordero)
leg (of lamb)
pimentón
paprika
pimienta
pepper
pimientos
green/red peppers
piña
pineapple
plancha (a la)
grilled
plátano
banana
plato principal
main course
platos típicos
regional specialities
pollo
chicken
puerro
leek
pulpo
octopus
queso
cheese
rábanos
radishes
rabo de buey
oxtail
rape
monkfish
remolacha
beetroot
riñones
kidneys
rodaballo
turbot
romana (a la)
deep fried
vino rosado
rosé wine
salchicha
sausage

salchichón
salami
salmón
salmon
salmón ahumado
smoked salmon
salmonete
red mullet
sandía
water melon
sangría
sangría
sardinas
sardines
setas
mushrooms
solomillo de buey
fillet of beef
sopa
soup
tarta helada
ice cream cake
ternera
veal
tinto
red wine
tocino
bacon
tortilla española
Spanish omelette
  (potato)
tortilla francesa
plain omelette
tortitas
waffles
trucha
trout
trufas
truffles
turrón
nougat
uvas
grapes
verduras
green vegetables
vinagre
vinegar
zanahorias
carrots
zumo de naranja
orange juice

On the road

5 On the road

5 .1 Asking for directions

Excuse me, could I ask ____ you something?	Perdone, ¿podría preguntarle algo? *pehrdohneh, pohdreeah prehgoontahrleh ahlgoh?*
I've lost my way_____	Me he perdido *meh eh pehrdeedoh*
Is there a(n)... _____ around here?	¿Sabe dónde hay un(a)...por aqui? *sahbeh dohndeh ay oon(ah)...pohr ahkee?*
Is this the way to...? _____	¿Se va por aquí a...? *seh bah pohr ahkee ah...?*
Could you tell me _____ how to get to the... (name of place) by car/on foot?	¿Podría decirme cómo llegar a... (en coche/a pie)? *pohdreeah dehtheermeh kohmoh lyehgahr ah... (ehn kohcheh/ah pyeh)?*
What's the quickest_____ way to...?	¿Cómo hago para llegar lo antes posible a...? *kohmoh ahgoh pahrah lyehgahr loh ahntehs pohseebleh ah...?*
How many kilometres ____ is it to...?	¿Cuántos kilómetros faltan para llegar a...? *kwahntohs keelohmehtrohs fahltahn pahrah lyehgahr ah...?*
Could you point it _____ out on the map?	¿Podría señalarlo en el mapa? *pohdreeah sehnyahlahrloh ehn ehl mahpah?*

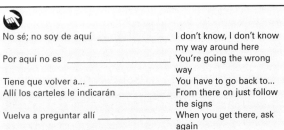

No sé; no soy de aquí _____	I don't know, I don't know my way around here
Por aquí no es _____	You're going the wrong way
Tiene que volver a... _____	You have to go back to...
Allí los carteles le indicarán _____	From there on just follow the signs
Vuelva a preguntar allí _____	When you get there, ask again

todo recto straight ahead	la calle the street	el viaducto the fly-over
a la izquierda left	el semáforo the traffic light	el puente the bridge
a la derecha right	el túnel the tunnel	el paso a nivel/las barreras
doblar turn	el stop the `give way' sign	the level crossing/the boom gates
seguir follow	el edificio the building	el cartel en dirección de...
cruzar cross	en la esquina at the corner	the sign pointing to...
el cruce the intersection	el río the river	la flecha the arrow

.2 Customs

● **Border documents**: valid passport, visa. For car and motorbike: valid UK driving licence and registration document, insurance document, green card, UK registration plate.
Import and export specifications:
– Foreign currency: no restrictions
– Alcohol: 10 litres of spirits and 90 litres of wine. Tobacco: 800 cigarettes, 200 cigars or a kilo of tobacco. Restricted to personal consumption only.

Su pasaporte, por favor _____	Your passport, please
La tarjeta verde, por favor _____	Your green card, please
El permiso de circulación/la carta _____ gris, por favor	Your vehicle documents, please
¿Adónde va? _____	Where are you heading?
¿Cuánto tiempo piensa quedarse? _____	How long are you planning to stay?
¿Tiene algo que declarar? _____	Do you have anything to declare?
¿Puede abrir esto? _____	Open this, please

My children are entered ___ on this passport	Mis hijos están apuntados en este pasaporte *mees ee<u>h</u>ohs ehstahn ahpoontahdohs ehn ehsteh pahsahpohrteh*
I'm travelling through _____	Estoy de paso *ehstoy deh pahsoh*
I'm going on holiday to... __	Voy de vacaciones a... *boy deh bahkahthyohnehs ah...*
I'm on a business trip _____	He venido en viaje de negocios *eh behneedoh en byah<u>h</u>eh deh nehgohthyohs*
I don't know how long _____ I'll be staying yet	Todavía no sé cuánto tiempo me quedaré *tohdahbeeah noh seh kwahntoh tyehmpoh meh kehdahreh*
I'll be staying here for _____ a weekend	Pienso quedarme un fin de semana *pyehnsoh kehdahrmeh oon feen deh sehmahnah*
– for a few days _____	Pienso quedarme unos días *pyehnsoh kehdahrmeh oonohs deeahs*
– for a week_____	Pienso quedarme una semana *pyehnsoh kehdahrmeh oonah sehmahnah*
– for two weeks _____	Pienso quedarme dos semanas *pyehnsoh kehdahrmeh dohs sehmahnahs*
I've got nothing to_____ declare	No tengo nada que declarar *noh tehngoh nahdah keh dehklahrahr*
I've got...with me_____	Traigo... *trahygoh...*
– ...cartons of cigarettes ___	Traigo...cartones de cigarrillos *trahygoh...kahrtohnehs deh theegahrreelyohs*
– ...bottles of... _____	Traigo...botellas de... *trahygoh...bohtehlyahs deh...*

On the road

5

45

– some souvenirs _____	Traigo algunos recuerdos de viaje
	trahygoh ahlgoonohs rehkwehrdohs de byahheh
These are personal _____ effects	Estos son artículos personales
	ehstohs sohn ahrteekoolohs pehrsohnahlehs
These are not new _____	Estas cosas no son nuevas
	ehstahs kohsahs noh sohn nwehbahs
Here's the receipt _____	Aquí está el recibo
	ahkee ehstah ehl rehtheeboh
This is for private use _____	Esto es para uso personal
	ehstoh ehs pahrah oosoh pehrsohnahl
How much import duty ____ do I have to pay?	¿Cuánto tengo que pagar por derechos de aduana?
	kwahntoh tehngoh keh pahgahr pohr dehrehchohs deh ahdwahnah?
Can I go now? _____	¿Puedo seguir?
	pwehdoh sehgheer?

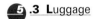

5 .3 Luggage

Porter! _____	¡Mozo!
	mohthoh!
Could you take this _____ luggage to...?	¿Podría llevar este equipaje a...?
	pohdreeah lyehbahr ehsteh ehkeepahheh ah...?
How much do I _____ owe you?	¿Cuánto le debo?
	kwahntoh leh dehboh?
Where can I find a _____ luggage trolley?	¿Dónde hay carritos para el equipaje?
	dohndeh ay kahrreetohs pahrah ehl ehkeepahheh?
Could you store this _____ luggage for me?	¿Podría dejar este equipaje en la consigna?
	pohdreeah dehhahr ehsteh ehkeepahheh ehn lah kohnseegnah?
Where are the luggage _____ lockers?	¿Dónde está la consigna automática?
	dohndeh ehstah lah kohnseegnah ahootohmahteekah?
I can't get the locker _____ open	No logro abrir la puerta de la consigna
	noh lohgroh ahbreer lah pwehrtah deh lah kohnseegnah
How much is it per item ___ per day?	¿Cuánto sale por bulto y por día?
	kwahntoh sahleh pohr booltoh ee pohr deeah?
This is not my bag/_____ suitcase	Este/ésta no es mi bolso/mi maleta
	ehsteh/ehstah noh ehs mee bohlsoh/mee mahlehtah
There's one item/bag/ _____ suitcase missing still	Todavía falta un bulto/un bolso/una maleta
	tohdahbeeah fahltah oon booltoh/oon bohlsoh/oonah mahlehtah
My suitcase is damaged ___	Me han dañado la maleta
	meh ahn dahnyahdoh lah mahlehtah

a la derecha	ceda el paso	obras
right	give way	roadworks ahead
a la izquierda	cerrado	paso a nivel
left	closed	(sin barreras)
abierto	cruce peligroso	level crossing
open	dangerous crossing	(no gates)
altura máxima	curvas en ... km	paso de ganado
maximum height	bends for...km	cattle crossing
arcenes sin afirmar	despacio	peaje
soft verges	drive slowly	toll
¡atención, peligro!	desprendimientos	peatones
danger	loose rocks	pedestrian crossing
autopista de peaje	desvío	precaución
toll road	diversion	caution
autovía	dirección prohibida	prohibido aparcar
motorway	no entry	no parking
bajada peligrosa	dirección única	prohibido adelantar
steep hill	one-way traffic	no overtaking
calzada resbaladiza	encender las luces	puesto de socorro
slippery road	switch on lights	first aid
cambio de sentido	espere	salida
change of direction	wait	exit
cañada	estacionamiento	salida de camiones
animals crossing	reglamentado	factory/works exit
carretera comarcal	limited parking zone	substancias
secondary road	excepto...	peligrosas
carretera cortada	except for...	dangerous
road closed	fin de...	substances
carretera en mal	end of...	travesía peligrosa
estado	hielo	dangerous crossing
irregular road	ice on road	zona peatonal
surface	niebla	pedestrian zone
carretera nacional	beware fog	
main road		

 .5 The car

See the diagram on page 51.

● **The motorways in Spain** have been very well updated and expanded. Tolls, however, can be expensive.

Particular traffic regulations:
maximum speed for cars:
120km/h on toll roads
110km/h on other motorways
60km/h in town centres
– give way: all traffic from the right has the right of way, except for major roads and thoroughfares.
– towing: prohibited to private drivers.

5.6 The petrol station

● **Petrol is easily available** but rather expensive in Spain.

How many kilometres to ___ the next petrol station, please?	¿Cuántos kilómetros faltan para la próxima gasolinera? *kwahntohs keelohmehtrohs fahltahn pahrah lah prohxeemah gahsohleenehrah?*
I would like...litres of..., ___ please	Póngame...litros de..., por favor *pohngahmeh...leetrohs deh..., pohr fahbohr*
– super _____	Póngame...litros de gasolina súper *pohngahmeh...leetrohs de gahsohleenah soopehr*
– leaded _____	Póngame...litros de gasolina normal *pohngahmeh...leetrohs deh gahsohleenah nohrmahl*
– unleaded_____	Póngame...litros de gasolina sin plomo *pohngahmeh...leetrohs deh gahsohleenah seen plohmoh*
– diesel _____	Póngame...litros de gasóleo *pohngahmeh...leetrohs deh gahsohlehoh*
I would like...pesetas' _____ worth of petrol, please	Póngame gasolina por...pesetas *pohngahmeh gahsohleenah pohr...pehsehtahs*
Fill her up, please _____	Lléneme el depósito, por favor *lyehnehmeh ehl dehpohseetoh, pohr fahvohr*
Could you check...?_____	¿Podría controlar...? *pohdreeah kohntrohlahr?*
– the oil level _____	¿Podría controlar el nivel del aceite? *pohdreeah kohntrohlahr ehl neebehl dehl ahtheheeteh?*
– the tyre pressure _____	¿Podría controlar la presión de los neumáticos? *pohdreeah kohntrohlahr lah prehsyohn deh lohs nehoomahteekohs?*
Could you change the _____ oil, please?	¿Podría cambiar el aceite? *pohdreeah kahmbyahr ehl atheheeteh?*
Could you clean the _____ windows/the windscreen, please?	¿Podría limpiar los cristales/el parabrisas? *pohdreeah leempyahr lohs kreestahlehs/ehl pahrahbreesahs?*
Could you give the car____ a wash, please?	¿Podría lavar el coche? *pohdreeah lahbahr ehl kohcheh?*

On the road

I'm having car trouble. Could you give me a hand?	Tengo una avería. ¿Podría ayudarme? *tehngoh oonah ahbehreeah. pohdreeah ahyoodahrmeh?*
I've run out of petrol	Me he quedado sin gasolina *meh eh kehdahdoh seen gahsohleenah*
I've locked the keys in the car	Me he dejado las llaves en el coche *meh eh dehhahdoh lahs lyabehs ehn ehl kohcheh*
The car/motorbike/ moped won't start	El coche/la moto/el ciclomotor no arranca *ehl kohcheh/lah mohtoh/ehl theeklohmohtohr noh ahrrahnkah*
Could you contact the recovery service for me, please?	¿Podría avisar al auxilio en carretera? *pohdreeah ahbeesar ahl ahooxeelyoh ehn kahrrehtehrah?*
Could you call a garage for me, please?	¿Podría llamar por teléfono a un taller mecánico? *pohdreeah lyahmahr pohr tehlehfohnoh ah oon tahlyehr mehkahneekoh?*
Could you give me a lift to...?	¿Me podría llevar a...? *meh pohdreeah lyehbar ah...?*
– a garage/into town?	¿Me podría llevar a un taller mecánico/a la ciudad? *meh pohdreeah lyehbar ah oon tahlyehr mehkahneekoh/ah lah thyoodahdh?*
– a phone booth?	¿Me podría llevar a una cabina de teléfonos? *meh pohdreeah lyehbar ah oonah kahbeenah deh tehlehfohnohs?*
– an emergency phone?	¿Me podría llevar a un teléfono de emergencia? *meh pohdreeah lyehbar ah oon tehlehfohnoh deh ehmehrhehnthyah?*
Can we take my bicycle/moped?	¿Podríamos llevar la bicicleta/el ciclomotor? *pohdreeahmohs lyehbar lah beetheeklehtah/ehl theeklohmohtohr?*
Could you tow me to a garage?	¿Podría remolcarme hasta un taller mecánico? *pohdreeah rehmohlkahrmeh ahstah oon tahlyehr mehkahneekoh?*
There's probably something wrong with...(See 5.8).	Me parece que está fallando el/la... *meh pahrehtheh keh ehstah fahlyahndoh ehl/lah...*
Can you fix it?	¿Podría arreglarlo? *pohdreeah ahrrehglahrloh?*
Could you fix my tyre?	¿Podría arreglar el neumático? *pohdreeah ahrrehglahr ehl nehoomahteekoh?*
Could you change this wheel?	¿Podría cambiar esta rueda? *pohdreeah kahmbyahr ehstah rwehdah?*

On the road

49

The parts of a car

(the diagram shows the numbered parts)

1 battery	la batería	*lah bahtehreeah*
2 rear light	el faro piloto	*ehl fahroh peelohtoh*
3 rear-view mirror	el retrovisor	*ehl rehtrohbeesohr*
reversing light	la luz de marcha atrás	*lah looth deh mahrchah ahtrahs*
4 aerial	la antena	*lah ahntehnah*
car radio	la autorradio	*lah ahootohrrahdyoh*
5 petrol tank	el depósito de gasolina	*ehl dehpohseetoh deh gahsohleenah*
inside mirror	el espejo interior	*ehl ehspehhoh eentehreeohr*
6 sparking plugs	las bujías	*lahs booheeahs*
fuel filter/pump	el separador de gasolina	*ehl sehpahrahdohr deh gahsohleenah*
7 wing mirror	el espejo exterior	*ehl ehspehoh ehxtehryohr*
8 bumper	el parachoques	*ehl pahrahchohkehs*
carburettor	el carburador	*ehl kahrboorahdohr*
crankcase	el cárter	*ehl kahrtehr*
cylinder	el cilindro	*ehl theeleendroh*
ignition	los contactos del ruptor	*lohs kohntahktohs dehl rooptohr*
warning light	la luz piloto	*lah looth peelohtoh*
dynamo	la dinamo	*lah deenahmoh*
accelerator	el pedal del acelerador	*ehl pehdahl dehl ahtehlehrahdohr*
handbrake	el freno de mano	*ehl frehnoh deh mahnoh*
valve	la válvula	*lah bahlboolah*
9 silencer	el silenciador	*ehl seelehnthyahdohr*
10 boot	el maletero	*ehl mahlehtehroh*
11 headlight	el faro	*ehl fahroh*
crank shaft	el cigueñal	*ehl theegwehnyahl*
12 air filter	el filtro de aire	*ehl feeltroh deh ayreh*
fog lamp	la luz antiniebla trasera	*lah looth ahnteenyehblah trahsehrah*
13 engine block	el bloque motor	*ehl blohkeh mohtohr*
camshaft	el árbol de levas	*ehl ahrbohl deh lehbahs*
oil filter/pump	el filtro de aceite	*ehl feeltroh deh ahtheheeteh*
dipstick	la varilla indicadora de nivel de aceite	*lah bahreelyah eendeekahdohrah deh neebehl deh ahtheyteh*
pedal	el pedal	*ehl pehdahl*
14 door	la portezuela	*lah pohrtehthwehlah*
15 radiator	el radiador	*ehl rahdyahdohr*
16 brake disc	el disco del freno	*ehl deeskoh dehl frehnoh*
spare wheel	la rueda de reserva	*lah rwehdah deh rehsehrbah*
17 indicator	el intermitente	*ehl eentehrmeetehnteh*
steering wheel	el volante	*ehl bohlahnteh*
18 windscreen wiper	el limpiaparabrisas	*ehl leempyahpahrahbreesahs*
19 shock absorbers	los amortiguadores	*lohs ahmohrteegwahdohrehs*
sunroof	el techo corredizo	*ehl tehchoh kohrrehdeethoh*
spoiler	el spoiler	*ehl spoheelehr*
starter motor	el motor de arranque	*ehl mohtohr deh ahrrahnkeh*

On the road — 5

20	steering column	el cárter de la dirección	*ehl kahrtehr deh lah deerehkthyohn*
21	exhaust pipe	el tubo de escape	*ehl tooboh deh ehskahpeh*
22	seat belt	el cinturón de seguridad	*ehl theentoorohn deh sehgooreedahdh*
	fan	el ventilador	*ehl behnteelahdohr*
23	distributor cables	los cables del distribuidor	*lohs kahblehs dehl deestreebweedohr*
24	gear lever	la palanca de cambios	*lah pahlahnkah deh kahmbyohs*
25	windscreen water pump	el parabrisas	*ehl pahrahbreesahs*
		la bomba de agua	*lah bohmbah deh ahgwah*
26	wheel	la rueda	*lah rwehdah*
27	hubcap	el tapacubos	*ehl tahpahkoobohs*
	piston	el émbolo	*ehl ehmbohloh*

Can you fix it so it'll get me to...?	¿Podría arreglarlo de tal manera que pueda seguir hasta...?
	pohdreeah ahrrehglahrloh deh tahl mahnehrah keh pwehdah sehgheer ahstah...?
Which garage can help me?	¿En qué taller me podrán ayudar entonces?
	ehn keh tahlyehr meh pohdrahn ahyoodahr ehntohnthehs?
When will my car/bicycle be ready?	¿Para cuándo estará mi coche/bicicleta?
	pahrah kwahndoh ehstahrah mee kohcheh/beetheeklehtah?
Can I wait for it here?	¿Puedo esperar aquí?
	pwehdoh ehspehrahr ahkee?
How much will it cost?	¿Por cuánto me va a salir?
	pohr kwahntoh meh bah ah sahleer?
Could you itemise the bill?	¿Podría especificar la cuenta?
	pohdreeah ehspehtheefeekahr lah kwehntah?
Can I have a receipt for the insurance?	¿Me podría dar un recibo para el seguro?
	meh pohdreeah dahr oon rehtheeboh pahrah ehl sehgooroh?

.8 The bicycle/moped

See the diagram on page 55.

● **Cycle paths** are rare in Spain. Not much consideration for bikes should be expected on the roads. The maximum speed for mopeds is 40km/h both inside and outside town centres. A helmet is compulsory.

No tengo piezas de recambio para su coche/su bicicleta	I don't have parts for your car/bicycle
Las piezas de recambio me las tienen que traer de otro sitio	I have to get the parts from somewhere else
Las piezas de recambio tengo que encargarlas	I have to order the parts
Eso llevará medio día	That'll take half a day
Eso llevará un día	That'll take a day
Eso llevará unos días	That'll take a few days
Eso llevará una semana	That'll take a week
Su coche ha quedado totalmente destruido	Your car is a write-off
Ya no se puede hacer nada para arreglarlo	It can't be repaired
El coche/la moto/el ciclomotor/la bicicleta estará para las...	The car/motor bike/moped/bicycle will be ready at... o'clock

I'd like to rent a...	Quisiera alquilar un...
	keesyehrah ahlkeelahr oon...
Do I need a (special) licence for that?	¿Hace falta un permiso de conducir (especial)?
	ahteh fahltah oon pehrmeesoh deh kohndootheer (ehspehthyahl)?
I'd like to rent the...for...	Quisiera alquilar el/la...por...
	keesyehrah ahlkeelahr ehl/lah...pohr...
– one day	Quisiera alquilar el/la...por un día
	keesyehrah ahlkeelahr ehl/lah...pohr oon deeah
– two days	Quisiera alquilar el/la...por dos días
	keesyehrah ahlkeelahr ehl/lah...pohr dohs deeahs
How much is that per day/week?	¿Cuánto sale por día/semana?
	kwahntoh sahleh pohr deeah/pohr sehmahnah?
How much is the deposit?	¿Cuánto es la fianza?
	kwahntoh ehs lah fyahnthah?
Could I have a receipt for the deposit?	¿Me podría dar un recibo por el pago de la fianza?
	meh pohdreeah dahr oon rehtheeboh pohr ehl pahgoh deh lah fyahnthah?
How much is the surcharge per kilometre?	¿Cuánto hay que pagar extra por kilómetro?
	kwahntoh ay keh pahgahr ehxtrah pohr keelohmehtroh?
Does that include petrol?	¿Está incluida la gasolina?
	ehstah eenklooeedah lah gahsohleenah?
Does that include insurance?	¿Está incluido el seguro?
	ehstah eenklooeedoh ehl sehgooroh?
What time can I pick the...up tomorrow?	¿A qué hora puedo pasar mañana a buscar el/la...?
	ah keh ohrah pwehdoh pahsahr mahnyahnah ah booskahr ehl/lah...?
When does the...have to be back?	¿A qué hora tengo que devolver el/la...?
	ah keh ohrah tehngoh keh dehbohlbehr ehl/lah...?
Where's the petrol tank?	¿Dónde está el depósito de gasolina?
	dohndeh ehstah ehl dehpohseetoh deh gahsohleenah?
What sort of fuel does it take?	¿Qué tipo de combustible hay que echarle?
	keh teepoh deh kohmboosteebleh ay keh ehchahrleh?

5 .10 **Hitchhiking**

Where are you heading?	¿Adónde va?
	ahdohndeh bah?
Can I come along?	¿Me podría llevar?
	meh pohdreeah lyehbahr?
Can my boyfriend/ girlfriend come too?	¿Podría llevar también a mi amigo/amiga?
	pohdreeah lyehbahr tahmbyehn ah mee ahmeegoh/ahmeegah?

On the road

The parts of a bicycle

(the diagram shows the numbered parts)

1	rear lamp	el piloto	*ehl peelohtoh*
2	rear wheel	la rueda trasera	*lah rwehdah trahsehrah*
3	(luggage) carrier	el portaequipajes	*ehl pohrtahehkeepahhehs*
4	bicycle fork	la cabeza	*lah kahbehthah*
5	bell	el timbre	*ehl teembreh*
	inner tube	la cámara	*lah kahmahrah*
	tyre	el neumático/la cubierta	*ehl nehoomahteekoh/lah koobyehrtah*
6	crank	la biela	*lah byehlah*
7	gear change	el cambio de velocidades	*ehl kahmbyoh deh behlotheedahdehs*
	wire	el hilo	*ehl eeloh*
	dynamo	la dinamo	*lah deenahmoh*
	bicycle trailer	el remolque de bicicleta	*ehl rehmohlkeh deh beetheeklehtah*
	frame	el cuadro	*ehl kwahdroh*
8	dress guard	el guardafaldas	*ehl gwardahfahldahs*
9	chain	la cadena de rodillos	*lah kahdehnah deh rohdeelyohs*
	chain guard	el cubrecadena/el cárter	*ehl koobrehkahdehnah/ehl kahrtehr*
	chain lock	la cadena antirrobo	*lah kahdehnah ahnteerrohboh*
	milometer	el contador kilométrico	*ehl kohntahdohr keelohmehtreekoh*
	child's seat	el sillín para niños	*ehl seelyeen pahrah neenyohs*
10	headlamp	el faro	*ehl fahroh*
	bulb	la bombilla	*lah bohmbeelyah*
11	pedal	el pedal	*ehl pehdahl*
12	pump	la bombilla	*lah bohmbeelyah*
13	reflector	el cristal reflectante	*ehl kreestahl rehflehktahnteh*
14	brake pad	la zapatilla del freno	*lah thahpahteelyah dehl frehnoh*
15	brake cable	el cable del freno	*ehl kahbleh dehl frehnoh*
16	ring lock	la cerradura	*lah thehrrahdoorah*
17	carrier straps	las bandas elásticas	*lahs bahndahs ehlahsteekahs*
18	spoke	el radio/el rayo	*ehl rahdyoh/ehl rahyoh*
19	mudguard	el guardabarros	*ehl gwahrdahbahrrohs*
20	handlebar	el manillar	*ehl mahneelyahr*
21	chain wheel	el piñón	*ehl peenyohn*
	toe clip	el calapiés	*ehl kahlahpyehs*
22	crank axle	el eje del cigüeñal	*ehl ehheh dehl theegwehnyal*
	drum brake	el freno de tambor	*ehl frehnoh deh tahmbohr*
23	tube	la llanta	*lah lyahntah*
24	valve	la válvula	*lah bahlboolah*
	valve tube	el tubo de la válvula	*ehl tooboh deh lah bahlboolah*

On the road 5

25 gear cable	el cable de velocidades	*ehl kahbleh deh behlohtheedahdehs*
26 fork	la horquilla	*lah ohrkeelyah*
27 front wheel	la rueda delantera	*lah rwehdah dehlahntehrah*
28 seat	el sillín	*el seelyeen*

I'm trying to get to...	Voy a... *boy ah...*
Is that on the way to...?	¿Eso está camino de...? *ehsoh ehstah kahmeenoh deh...?*
Could you drop me off...?	¿Me podría dejar...? *meh pohdreeah deh<u>h</u>ahr...?*
– here?	¿Me podría dejar aquí mismo? *meh pohdreeah deh<u>h</u>ahr ahkee meesmoh?*
– at the...exit?	¿Me podría dejar en la salida de...? *meh pohdreeah deh<u>h</u>ahr ehn lah sahleedah deh...?*
– in the centre?	¿Me podría dejar en el centro? *meh pohdreeah deh<u>h</u>ahr ehn ehl thehntroh?*
– at the next roundabout?	¿Me podría dejar en la próxima rotonda? *meh pohdreeah deh<u>h</u>ahr ehn lah prohxeemah rohtohndah?*
Could you stop here, please?	¿Podría pararse aquí? *pohdreeah pahrahrseh ahkee?*
I'd like to get out here	Quisiera bajarme aquí *keesyehrah bah<u>h</u>ahrmeh ahkee*
Thanks for the lift	Gracias por llevarme *grahthyahs pohr lyehbahrmeh*

On the road

5

Public transport

6 **P**ublic transport

6.1 **I**n general

● **The rail network** has been substantially overhauled and expanded and there is now a good, fast service available with the Talgo and Ave in the south. These trains require payment of a supplement and it is advisable to reserve seats in advance, at the station or at travel agencies. Tickets for buses and the metro can be bought at an *estanco*, as well as metro stations.

Announcements

El tren [de las 10:40] con destino a..., ___ ..., saldrá con (unos)...minutos de retraso	The [10:40] train to...has been delayed by 15 minutes
Por la vía 5 entrará el tren _____ [de las 10:40] con destino a.../ procedente de...	The train now arriving at platform 5 is the [10:40] train to .../from...
En la vía 5 está por partir el tren _____ [de las 10:40]...	The [10:40] train to...is about to leave from platform 5
Su atención, por favor _____ Manténganse lejos de la vía; un tren Intercity pasará por la plataforma...	Attention please! Keep your distance from the rail track, an intercity train will pass on platform...
Nos estamos aproximando a la _____ estación de...	We're now approaching...

Where does this train go to?	¿Adónde va este tren? *ahdohndeh bah ehsteh trehn?*
Does this boat go to...?	¿Este barco va a...? *ehsteh bahrkoh bah ah...?*
Can I take this bus to...?	¿Puedo coger este autobús para ir a...? *pwehdoh koh<u>h</u>ehr ehsteh ahootohboos pahrah eer ah...?*
Does this train stop at...?	¿Este tren para en...? *ehsteh trehn pahrah ehn...?*
Is this seat taken/free /reserved?	¿Está ocupado/libre/reservado este asiento? *ehstah ohkoopahdoh/leebreh/rehsehrbahdoh ehsteh ahsyehntoh?*
I've booked...	He reservado... *eh rehsehrbahdoh...*
Could you tell me where I have to get off for... ?	¿Me podría decir dónde me tengo que bajar para ir a...? *meh pohdreeah dehtheer dohndeh meh tehngoh keh bah<u>h</u>ar pahrah eer ah...?*
Could you let me know when we get to...?	¿Me podría avisar cuando lleguemos a...? *meh pohdreeah ahbeesahr kwahndoh lyehghehmohs ah...?*
Could you stop at the next stop, please?	La próxima parada, por favor *lah prohxeemah pahrahdah pohr fahbohr*

Public transport

Where are we now? _____	¿Dónde estamos?
	dohndeh ehstahmohs?
Do I have to get off here? __	¿Tengo que bajarme aquí?
	tehngoh keh bahhahrmeh ahkee?
Have we already _____ passed...?	¿Ya hemos pasado...?
	yah ehmohs pahsahdoh...?
How long have I been _____ asleep?	¿Cuánto tiempo he dormido?
	kwahntoh tyehmpoh eh dohrmeedoh?
How long does... _____ stop here?	¿Cuánto tiempo se queda aquí...?
	kwahntoh tyehmpoh seh kehdah ahkee?
Can I come back on the____ same ticket?	¿Este billete me sirve para volver?
	ehsteh beelyehteh meh seerbeh pahrah bohlbehr?
Can I change on this_____ ticket?	¿Se puede hacer trasbordo con este billete?
	seh pwehdeh ahtehehr trahsbohrdoh kohn ehsteh beelyehteh?
How long is this ticket _____ valid for?	¿Hasta cuándo es válido este billete?
	ahstah kwahndoh ehs bahleedoh ehsteh beelyehteh
How much is the _____ supplement for the Talgo/Ave (high speed train)?	¿Cuánto vale el suplemento para el Talgo/el Ave?
	kwahntoh bahleh ehl sooplehmehntoh pahrah ehl tahlgoh/ehl ahbeh?

6 .2 Questions to passengers

Ticket types

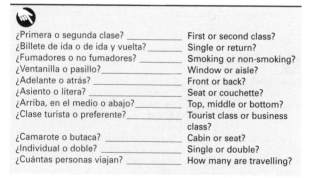

¿Primera o segunda clase? _____	First or second class?
¿Billete de ida o de ida y vuelta? _____	Single or return?
¿Fumadores o no fumadores? _____	Smoking or non-smoking?
¿Ventanilla o pasillo?_____	Window or aisle?
¿Adelante o atrás? _____	Front or back?
¿Asiento o litera? _____	Seat or couchette?
¿Arriba, en el medio o abajo?_____	Top, middle or bottom?
¿Clase turista o preferente?_____	Tourist class or business class?
¿Camarote o butaca? _____	Cabin or seat?
¿Individual o doble? _____	Single or double?
¿Cuántas personas viajan? _____	How many are travelling?

Public transport

6

Destination

¿Adónde quiere ir? _____	Where are you travelling?
¿Qué día sale? _____	When are you leaving?
Su...sale a las... _____	Your...leaves at...
Tiene que hacer trasbordo _____	You have to change trains
Tiene que bajarse en... _____	You have to get off at...
Tiene que pasar por... _____	You have to travel via...
El viaje de ida es el día... _____	The outward journey is on...
El viaje de vuelta es el día... _____	The return journey is on...
Tiene que embarcar a las...a _____ más tardar	You have to be on board by...

Inside the vehicle

Billetes, por favor _____	Your ticket, please
Su reserva, por favor _____	Your reservation, please
Su pasaporte, por favor _____	Your passport, please
Se ha equivocado de asiento _____	You're in the wrong seat
Se ha equivocado de... _____	You're on/in the wrong...
Este asiento está reservado _____	This seat is reserved
Tiene que pagar un suplemento _____	You'll have to pay a supplement
El...tiene un retraso de...minutos _____	The...has been delayed by...minutes

6 .3 Tickets

Where can I...? _____	¿Dónde...?
	dohndeh...?
– buy a ticket? _____	¿Dónde se compran los billetes?
	dohndeh seh kohmprahn lohs beelyehtehs?
– make a reservation? _____	¿Dónde se hacen las reservas?
	dohndeh seh ahthehn lahs rehsehrbahs?
– book a flight? _____	¿Dónde puedo hacer una reserva para un vuelo?
	dohndeh pwehdoh ahthehr oonah rehsehrbah pahrah oon bwehloh?
Could I have a...to..., please? _____	Quiero un/una...a...
	kyehroh oon/oonah...ah...
– a single _____	Quiero un billete de ida a...
	kyehroh oon beelyehteh deh eedah ah...
– a return _____	Quiero un billete de ida y vuelta a...
	kyehroh oon beelyehteh deh eedah ee bwehltah ah...
first class _____	en primera clase
	ehn preemehrah klahseh
second class _____	en segunda clase
	ehn sehgoondah klahseh

60

tourist class	en clase turista
	ehn klahseh tooreestah
business class	en clase preferente
	ehn klahseh prehfehrehnteh
I'd like to book a seat/couchette/cabin	Quisiera reservar un asiento/una litera/un camarote
	keesyehrah rehsehrbahr oon ahsyehntoh/oonah leetehrah/oon kahmahrohteh
I'd like to book a berth in the sleeping car	Quisiera reservar una plaza en un coche cama
	keesyehrah rehsehrbahr oonah plahthah ehn oon kohcheh kahmah
top/middle/bottom	arriba/en el medio/abajo
	ahrreebah/ehn ehl mehdyoh/ahbah<u>h</u>oh
smoking/no smoking	fumadores/no fumadores
	foomahdohrehs/noh foomahdohrehs
by the window	ventanilla
	behntahneelyah
single/double	individual/doble
	eendeebeedwahl/dohbleh
at the front/back	adelante/atrás
	ahdehlahnteh/ahtrahs
There are...of us	Somos...personas
	sohmohs...pehrsohnahs
a car	un coche
	oon kohcheh
a caravan	una caravana
	oonah kahrahbahnah
...bicycles	...bicicletas
	...beetheeklehtahs
Do you also have...?	¿Tienen...?
	tyehnehn...?
– season tickets?	¿Tienen billetes para varios viajes?
	tyehnehn beelyehtehs pahrah bahryohs byahhehs?
– weekly tickets?	¿Tienen abonos semanales?
	tyehnehn ahbohnohs sehmahnahlehs?
– monthly season tickets?	¿Tienen abonos mensuales?
	tyehnehn ahbohnohs mehnswahlehs?

Public transport

6.4 Information

Where's-?	¿Dónde hay...?
	dohndeh ay...?
Where's the information desk?	¿Dónde está la oficina de información?
	dohndeh ehstah lah ohfeetheenah deh eenfohrmahthyohn?
Where can I find a timetable?	¿Dónde hay un horario?
	dohndeh ay oon ohrahryoh?
Where's the...desk?	¿Dónde está el mostrador de...?
	dohndeh ehstah ehl mohstrahdohr deh...?
Do you have a city map with the bus/the underground routes on it?	¿Tendría un plano de la ciudad con la red de autobuses/metro?
	tehndreeah oon plahnoh deh lah thyoodahdh kohn lah rehth deh ahootohboosehs/mehtroh?

61

Do you have a _____ timetable?	¿Tendría un horario? *tehndreeah oon ohrahryoh?*
I'd like to confirm/_____ cancel/change my booking for/trip to...	Quisiera confirmar/cancelar/cambiar mi reserva/mi viaje a... *keesyehrah kohnfeermahr/kahnthehlahr/kahmbyahr mee rehsehrbah/mee byahhheh ah...*
Will I get my money _____ back?	¿Me devuelven el dinero? *meh dehbwehlbehn ehl deenehroh?*
I want to go to... _____ How do I get there? (What's the quickest way there?)	Tengo que ir a...¿Cómo hago para llegar (lo más rápido posible)? *tehngoh keh eer ah...kohmoh ahgoh pahrah lyehgahr(loh mahs rahpeedoh pohseebleh)?*
How much is a _____ single/return to...?	¿Cuánto vale un billete de ida/de ida y vuelta a...? *kwahntoh bahleh oon beelyehteh deh eedah ee bwehltah ah...?*
Do I have to pay a _____ supplement?	¿Tengo que pagar algún suplemento? *tehngoh keh pahgahr ahlgoon sooplehmehntoh?*
Can I interrupt my _____ journey with this ticket?	¿Con este billete puedo hacer una parada intermedia? *kohn ehsteh beelyehteh pwehdoh ahthehr oonah pahrahdah eentehrmehdyah?*
How much luggage _____ am I allowed?	¿Cuánto equipaje puedo llevar? *kwahntoh ehkeepahhheh pwehdoh lyebahr?*
Can I send my luggage _____ in advance?	¿Puedo enviar mi equipaje por anticipado? *pwehdoh ehnbeeahr mee ehkeepahhheh pohr ahnteetheepahdoh?*
Does this...travel direct? ___	¿Este...va directo? *ehsteh...bah deerehktoh?*
Do I have to change? _____ Where?	¿Tengo que hacer trasbordo? ¿Dónde? *tehngoh keh ahthehr trahsbohrdoh? dohndeh?*
Will there be any _____ stopovers?	¿Habrá escalas? *ahbrah ehskahlahs?*
Does the boat call in at ___ any ports on the way?	¿El barco hace alguna escala? *ehl bahrkoh ahtheh ahlgoonah ehskahlah?*
Does the train/ _____ bus stop at...?	¿Este tren/este autobús para en...? *ehsteh trehn/ehsteh ahootohboos pahrah ehn...?*
Where should I get off? ____	¿Dónde me tengo que bajar? *dohndeh meh tehngoh keh bahhhahr?*
Is there a connection _____ to...?	¿Hay enlace para...? *ay ehnlahtheh pahrah...?*
How long do I have to _____ wait?	¿Cuánto tengo que esperar? *kwahntoh tehngoh keh ehspehrahr?*
When does...leave? _____	¿Cuándo sale...? *kwahndoh sahleh...?*
What time does the _____ first/next/last...leave?	¿A qué hora sale el primer/próximo/último...? *ah keh ohrah sahleh ehl preemehr/prohxeemoh/oolteemoh...?*
How long does...take? ____	¿Cuánto tarda...en llegar? *kwahntoh tahrdah...ehn lyehgahr?*

What time does...arrive in...?	¿A qué hora llega...a...?
	ah keh ohrah lyegah...ah...?
Where does the...to... leave from?	¿De dónde sale el...a...?
	deh dohndeh sahleh ehl...ah...?
Is this...to...?	¿Este es...a...?
	ehsteh ehs...ah...?

6 .5 Aeroplanes

● **On arrival** at a Spanish airport, you will find the following signs:

llegadas	salidas
arrivals	departures

6 .6 Trains

● **The rail network** is very extensive, run by the RENFE (Red Nacional de Ferrocarriles Españoles). Some local trains are still rather slow so it is preferable to stipulate Talgo or Rápido when buying tickets. During the summer and before public holidays it is advisable to buy train tickets well in advance. Porters are few and far between.

6 .7 Taxis

● **There are plenty of taxis** in most cities. Supplements are payable for luggage and travel to stations or airports. It is advisable to inquire about the price in advance and make sure that you are hiring a city taxi.

libre	ocupado	parada de taxis
for hire	booked	taxi rank

Taxi!	¡Taxi!
	tahxee!
Could you get me a taxi, please?	¿Me podría llamar un taxi?
	meh pohdreeah lyahmahr oon tahksee?
Where can I find a taxi around here?	¿Dónde se puede coger un taxi por aquí?
	dohndeh seh pwehdeh kohhehr oon tahxee pohr ahkee?
Could you take me to..., please?	A..., por favor
	ah..., pohr fahbohr
– this address	A esta dirección, por favor
	ah ehstah deerehkthyohn, pohr fahbohr
– the...hotel	Al hotel..., por favor
	ahl ohtehl..., pohr fahbohr
– the town/city centre	Al centro, por favor
	ahl thehntroh, pohr fahbohr
– the station	A la estación, por favor
	ah lah ehstahthyohn, pohr fahbohr
– the airport	Al aeropuerto, por favor
	ahl ahehrohpwehrtoh, pohr fahbohr

How much is the _____ trip to...?	¿Cuánto sale el recorrido hasta...? *kwahntoh sahleh ehl rehkohrreedoh ahstah...?*
How far is it to...? _____	¿Cuánto es hasta...? *kwahntoh ehs ahstah...?*
Could you turn on the _____ meter, please?	¿Podría poner en marcha el taxímetro? *pohdreeah pohnehr ehn mahrchah ehl tahxeemehtroh?*
I'm in a hurry _____	Llevo prisa *lyehboh preesah*
Could you speed up/slow _ down a little?	¿Podría ir más rápido/más despacio? *pohdreeah eer mahs rahpeedoh/mahs dehspathyoh?*
Could you take a _____ different route?	¿Podría ir por otro camino? *pohdreeah eer pohr ohtroh kahmeenoh?*
I'd like to get out here, ____ please	Déjeme aquí *dehhehmeh ahkee*
You have to go...here _____	Siga...aquí *seegah...ahkee*
You have to go straight ___ on here	Siga todo recto aquí *seegah tohdoh rehktoh akee*
You have to turn left_____ here	Doble a la izquierda aquí *dohbleh ah lah eethkyehrdah ahkee*
You have to turn right ____ here	Doble a la derecha aquí *dohbleh ah lah dehrehchah ahkee*
This is it _____	Es aquí *ehs ahkee*
Could you wait a minute___ for me, please?	Espéreme un momentito, por favor *ehspehrehmeh oon mohmehnteetoh, pohr fahbohr*

Overnight accommodation

Overnight accommodation

7.1 General

● **There is great variety** in overnight accommodation in Spain.
It is advisable to book (and send confirmation) in advance.
Hotel: stars indicate the degree of comfort; from five stars, the most
luxurious, to one star, very basic. Most hotels offer *pensión completa*
(full board) or *media pensión* (half board).
Parador: Mainly, but not always, luxurious hotels in converted
castles or palaces in exceptional areas. These are very popular and
have to be booked very well in advance, but are well worth the visit.
They are under government supervision.
Hostal: Family run businesses for the most part, with one to three
stars. They do not always provide breakfast, but are clean and can be
very well situated.
Albergue: usually country inns.
Albergue de juventud: restricted to members of the international Youth
Hostels Association.
Camping: a list of sites can be found at any Tourist Office.

¿Cuánto tiempo piensa quedarse? _____	How long will you be staying?
Rellene este formulario, por favor _____	Fill in this form, please
¿Me permite su pasaporte? _____	Could I see your passport?
Tiene que pagar una fianza _____	I'll need a deposit
Tiene que pagar por adelantado_____	You'll have to pay in advance

My name's...I've made _____ a reservation over the phone/by mail	Me llamo...He reservado una habitación por teléfono/por carta *meh lyahmoh...eh rehsehrbahdoh oonah ahbeetahthyohn pohr tehlehfohnoh/pohr kahrtah*
How much is it per _____ night/week/ month?	¿Cuánto sale por noche/semana/mes? *kwahntoh sahleh pohr nohcheh/sehmahnah/mehs?*
We'll be staying at _____ least...nights/weeks	Pensamos quedarnos al menos...noches/semanas *pehnsahmohs kehdahrnohs ahl mehnohs...nohchehs/sehmahnahs*
We don't know yet _____	Todavía no lo sabemos exactamente *tohdahbeeah noh loh sahbehmohs ehxahktahmehnteh*
Do you allow pets _____ (cats/dogs)?	¿Están permitidos los animales domésticos (perros/gatos)? *ehstahn pehrmeeteedohs lohs ahneemahlehs dohmehsteekohs(pehrrohs/gahtohs)?*
What time does the _____ gate/door open/close?	¿A qué hora cierran/abren la verja/la puerta de entrada? *ah keh ohrah thyehrrahn/ahbrehn lah behrhah/lah pwehrtah deh ehntrahdah?*

Overnight accommodation

Could you get me _____ a taxi, please?	¿Podría llamar un taxi?
	pohdreeah lyahmahr oon tahxee?
Is there any mail _____ for me?	¿Hay carta para mí?
	ay kahrtah pahrah mee?

.2 Camping

See the diagram on page 69.

Puede elegir el sitio usted mismo _____	You can pick your own site
El sitio se lo asignamos nosotros _____	You'll be allocated a site
Este es el número de su _____ emplazamiento	This is your site number
Por favor pegue esto en el parabrisas ___ del coche	Stick this on your car, please
No pierda esta tarjeta _____	Please don't lose this card

Where's the manager? _____	¿Dónde está el encargado?
	dohnde ehstah ehl ehnkahrgahdoh?
Are we allowed to _____ camp here?	¿Podemos acampar aquí?
	pohdehmohs ahkahmpahr ahkee?
There are...of us and _____ ...tents	Somos...personas y...tiendas
	sohmohs...pehrsohnahs ee...tyehndahs
Can we pick our _____ own site?	¿Podemos elegir el sitio nosotros mismos?
	pohdehmohs ehle<u>h</u>heer ehl seetyoh nohsohtrohs meesmohs?
Do you have a quiet _____ spot for us?	¿Nos podría dar un sitio tranquilo?
	nohs pohdreeah dahr oon seetyoh trahnkeeloh?
Do you have any other ____ sites available?	¿No tiene otro sitio libre?
	noh tyehneh ohtroh seetyoh leebreh?
It's too windy/sunny/ _____ shady here.	Hay mucho viento/mucho sol/mucha sombra
	ay moochoh byehntoh/moochoh sohl/moochah sohmbrah
It's too crowded here _____	Hay mucha gente
	ay moochah <u>h</u>ehnteh
The ground's too _____ hard/uneven	El suelo es muy duro/muy desigual
	ehl swehloh ehs mwee dooroh/mwee dehseegwahl
Do you have a level _____ spot for the camper/caravan/folding caravan?	¿Tiene un sitio plano para el autocaravana/la caravana/el remolque tienda?
	tyehneh oon seetyoh plahnoh pahrah ehl ahootohkahrahbahnah/lah kahrahbahnah/ehl rehmohlkeh-tyehndah?
Could we have _____ adjoining sites?	¿Tiene dos plazas juntas?
	tyehneh dohs plahthahs <u>h</u>oontahs?
Can we park the car _____ next to the tent?	¿Podemos aparcar el coche junto a la tienda?
	pohdehmohs ahpahrkahr ehl kohcheh <u>h</u>oontoh ah lah tyehndah?

Camping equipment
(the diagram shows the numbered parts)

luggage space	el compartimiento de equipaje	*ehl kohmpahrteemyehntoh de ehkeepahheh*
can opener	el abrelatas	*ehl ahbrehlahtahs*
butane gas bottle	la bombona (de gas butano)	*lah bohmbohnah (deh gahs bootahnoh)*
1 pannier	la ciclobolsa	*lah theeklohbohlsah*
2 gas cooker	el hornillo de gas	*ehl ohrneelyoh deh gahs*
3 groundsheet	la lona del suelo	*lah lohnah dehl swehloh*
mallet	el martillo	*ehl mahrteelyoh*
hammock	la hamaca	*lah ahmahkah*
4 jerry can	el bidón	*ehl beedohn*
campfire	la fogata	*lah fohgahtah*
5 folding chair	la silla plegable	*lah seelyah plehgahbleh*
6 insulated picnic box	la nevera portátil/la bolsa nevera	*lah nehbehrah pohrtahteel/ lah bohlsah nehbehrah*
ice pack	el acumulador	*ehl akoomoolahdohr*
compass	la brújula	*lah broohoolah*
wick	la mecha	*lah mehchah*
corkscrew	el sacacorchos	*ehl sahkahkohrchohs*
7 airbed	el colchón neumático	*ehl kohlchohn nehoomahteekoh*
8 airbed plug	el taponcito de la válvula del colchón	*ehl tahpohntheetoh deh lah bahlboolah dehl kohlchohn*
pump	la bomba neumática	*lah bohmbah nehoomahteekah*
9 awning	el tejadillo	*ehl tehhahdeelyoh*
10 karimat	la esterilla	*lah ehstehreelyah*
11 pan	la olla	*lah ohlyah*
12 pan handle	el mango de la olla	*ehl mahngoh deh lah ohlyah*
primus stove	el hornillo de querosén	*ehl ohrneelyoh deh kehrohsehn*
zip	la cremallera	*lah krehmalyehrah*
13 backpack	la mochila	*lah mohcheelah*
14 guy rope	el viento	*ehl byehntoh*
sleeping bag	el saco de dormir	*ehl sahkoh deh dohrmeer*
15 storm lantern	el farol de tormentas	*ehl fahrohl deh tohrmehntahs*
camp bed	el catre (de tijera)	*ehl kahtreh (deh teehehrah)*
table	la mesa	*lah mehsah*
16 tent	la tienda	*lah tyehndah*
17 tent peg	la estaca	*lah ehstakah*
18 tent pole	el palo de tienda	*ehl pahloh deh tyehndah*
vacuum flask	el termo	*ehl tehrmoh*
19 water bottle	la cantimplora	*lah kahnteemplohrah*
clothes peg	la pinza	*lah peenthah*
clothes line	la cuerda de tender ropa	*lah kwehrdah deh tehndehr rohpah*
windbreak	el paravientos/el paraván	*ehl pahrahbyehntohs/ehl pahrahbahn*
20 torch	la linterna de bolsillo	*lah leentehrnah deh bohlseelyoh*
pocket knife	la navaja	*lah nahbahhah*

How much is it per person/tent/caravan/car?	¿Cuánto sale por persona/tienda/caravana/coche? *kwahntoh sahleh pohr pehrsohnah/tyehndah/ kahrahbahnah/kohcheh?*
Are there any...?	¿Hay...? *ay...?*
– any hot showers?	¿Hay duchas con agua caliente? *ay doochahs kohn ahgwah kahlyehnteh?*
– washing machines?	¿Hay lavadoras? *ay lahbahdohrahs?*
Is there a...on the site?	¿En este camping hay...? *ehn ehsteh kahmpeen ay...?*
Is there a children's play area on the site?	¿En este camping hay un sitio para que jueguen los niños? *ehn ehsteh kahmpeen ay oon seetyoh pahrah keh hwehghehn lohs neenyohs?*
Are there covered cooking facilities on the site?	¿En este camping hay un sitio cubierto para cocinar? *ehn ehsteh kahmpeen ay oon seetyoh koobyehrtoh pahrah kohtheenahr?*
Can I rent a safe here?	¿Tienen caja fuerte para alquilar? *tyehnehn kahhah fwehrteh pahrah ahlkeelahr?*
Are we allowed to barbecue here?	¿Se pueden hacer barbacoas? *seh pwehdehn ahtehr bahrbahkohahs?*
Are there any power points?	¿Hay tomas de corriente eléctrica? *ay tohmahs deh kohrryehnteh ehlehktreekah?*
Is there drinking water?	¿Hay agua potable? *ay ahgwah pohtahbleh?*
When's the rubbish collected?	¿Cuándo pasan a recoger la basura? *kwahndoh pahsahn ah rehkohhehr lah bahsoorah?*
Do you sell gas bottles (butane gas/propane gas)?	¿Venden bombonas de gas (butano/propano)? *behndehn bohmbohnahs deh gahs(bootahnoh/prohpahnoh)?*

7.3 Hotel/B&B/apartment/holiday house

Do you have a single/double room available?	¿Le queda alguna habitación individual/doble? *leh kehdah ahlgoonah ahbeetahthyohn eendeebeedwahl/dohbleh?*
per person/per room	por persona/por habitación *pohr pehrsohnah/pohr ahbeetahthyohn*
Does that include breakfast/lunch/dinner?	¿Incluye desayuno/comida/cena? *eenklooyeh dehsahyoonoh/kohmeedah/thehnah?*
Could we have two adjoining rooms?	¿Nos puede dar dos habitaciones una al lado de la otra? *nohs pwehdeh dahr dohs ahbeetahthyohnehs oonah ahl lahdoh deh lah ohtrah?*
with/without toilet/bath/shower	con/sin lavabo propio/baño propio/ducha propia *kohn/seen lahbahboh prohpyoh/bahnyoh prohpyo/doochah prohpyah?*

70

(not) facing the street _____	que (no) dé a la calle
	keh (noh) deh ah lah kahlyeh
with/without a view _____ of the sea	con/sin vista al mar
	kohn/seen beestah ahl mahr
Is there...in the hotel? _____	¿El hotel tiene...?
	ehl ohtehl tyehneh...?
Is there a lift in the _____ hotel?	¿El hotel tiene ascensor?
	ehl ohtehl tyehneh ahsthehnsohr?
Do you have room _____ service?	¿El hotel tiene servicio de habitación?
	ehl ohtehl tyehneh sehrbeethyoh deh ahbeetahthyohn?

Tiene lavabo y ducha en el mismo _____ piso/en su habitación	You can find the toilet and shower on the same floor/en suite
Por aquí, por favor _____	This way, please
Su habitación está en el...piso; es la_____ número...	Your room is on the...floor, number...

Could I see the room? _____	¿Puedo ver la habitación?
	pwehdoh behr lah habitathyohn?
I'll take this room_____	Me quedo con esta habitación
	meh kehdoh kohn ehstah abeetathyohn
We don't like this one _____	Esta no nos gusta
	ehstah noh nohs goostah
Do you have a larger/_____ less expensive room?	¿Tiene una habitación más grande/más barata?
	tyehneh oonah ahbeetathyohn mahs grahnde/mahs bahrahtah?
Could you put in a cot? _____	¿Puede agregar una cuna?
	pwehde ahgrehgahr oonah koonah?
What time's breakfast? _____	¿A qué hora es el desayuno?
	ah keh ohrah ehs ehl dehsahyoonoh?
Where's the dining _____ room?	¿Dónde está el comedor?
	dohndeh ehstah ehl kohmehdohr?
Can I have breakfast_____ in my room?	¿Me pueden traer el desayuno a la habitación?
	meh pwehdehn trahehr ehl dehsahyoonoh ah lah ahbeetahthyohn?
Where's the emergency_____ exit/fire escape?	¿Dónde está la salida de emergencia/la escalera de incendios?
	dohndeh ehstah lah sahleedah deh ehmehrrhehnthyah/lah ehskahlehrah de eentehndyohs?
Where can I park my _____ car (safely)?	¿Dónde hay un sitio (seguro) para aparcar el coche?
	dohndeh ay oon seetyoh sehgooroh pahrah ahpahrkahr ehl kohcheh?
The key to room..., _____ please	La llave de la habitación..., por favor
	lah lyahbeh deh lah ahbeetahthyohn..., pohr fahbohr
Could you put this in _____ the safe, please?	¿Podría dejar esto en la caja fuerte?
	pohdreeah dehhahr ehstoh ehn lah cahhah fwehrteh?

Could you wake me _____ at...tomorrow?	¿Me podría despertar mañana a las...?
	meh pohdreeah dehspehrtahr mahnyahnah ah lahs...?
Could you find a _____ babysitter for me?	¿Me podría conseguir una niñera para el bebé?
	meh pohdreeah kohnsehgeer oonah neenyehrah pahrah ehl behbeh?
Could I have an extra _____ blanket?	¿Tendría una manta extra?
	tehndreeah oonah mahntah ehxtrah?
What days do the _____ cleaners come in?	¿Qué días limpian la habitación?
	keh deeahs leempyahn lah ahbeetahthyohn?
When are the sheets/ _____ towels/tea towels changed?	¿Cuándo cambian las sábanas/las toallas/los paños de cocina?
	kwahndoh kahmbyahn lahs sahbahnahs/lahs tohahlyahs/lohs pahnyohs deh kohtheenah?

7 .4 **C**omplaints

We can't sleep for _____ the noise	No podemos dormir por el ruido
	noh pohdehmohs dohrmeer pohr ehl rweedoh
Could you turn the _____ radio down, please?	¿Podría bajar el volumen de la radio?
	pohdreeah bahhahr ehl vohloomehn deh lah rahdyoh?
We're out of toilet paper ___	Se ha acabado el papel higiénico.
	seh ah ahkahbahdoh ehl pahpehl eehyehneekoh
There aren't any.../ _____ there's not enough...	No hay.../no hay suficientes...
	noh ay.../noh ay soofeethyehntehs...
The bed linen's dirty_____	La ropa de cama está sucia
	lah rohpah deh kahmah ehstah soothyah
The room hasn't been _____ cleaned.	No han limpiado la habitación
	noh ahn leempyahdoh lah ahbeetahthyohn
The kitchen is not clean____	La cocina no está limpia
	lah kohtheenah noh ehstah leempyah
The kitchen utensils are____ dirty	Los utensilios de cocina están sucios
	lohs ootehnseelyohs deh kohtheenah ehstahn soothyohs
The heater's not_____ working	La calefacción no funciona
	lah kahlehfahkthyohn noh foonthyohnah
There's no (hot) _____ water/electricity	No hay agua (caliente)/electricidad
	noh ay ahgwah(kahlyehnteh)/ehlehktreetheedahdh
...is broken_____	...está estropeado
	...ehstah ehstrohpehahdoh
Could you have that _____ seen to?	¿Podrían hacerlo ver?
	pohdreeahn ahthehrloh behr?
Could I have another _____ room/site?	¿Tendría otra habitación/sitio para la tienda?
	tehndreeah ohtrah abeetahthyohn/seetyoh pahrah lah tyehndah?
The bed creaks terribly ____	La cama hace mucho ruido
	lah kahmah ahtheh moochoh rweedoh
The bed sags _____	La cama es demasiado blanda
	lah kahmah ehs dehmahsyahdoh blahndah

Overnight accommodation

There are bugs/insects____ in our room	Hay muchos bichos/insectos en nuestra habitación
	ay moochohs beechohs/eensehktohs ehn nwehstrah ahbeetahthyohn
This place is full_____ of mosquitos	Está lleno de mosquitos
	ehstah lyehnoh deh mohskeetohs
– cockroaches_____	Está lleno de cucarachas
	ehstah lyehnoh deh kookahrahchahs

.5 Departure

See also 8.2 Settling the bill

I'm leaving tomorrow.____ Could I settle my bill, please?	Mañana me voy. ¿Podría pagar la cuenta ahora?
	mahnyahnah meh boy. pohdreeah pahgahr lah kwehntah ahohrah?
What time should we_____ vacate?	¿A qué hora tenemos que dejar...?
	ah keh ohrah tehnehmohs keh deh__h__ahr...?
Could I have my_____ deposit/passport back, please?	¿Me devuelve la fianza/el pasaporte?
	meh dehbwehlbeh lah fyahnthah/ehl pahsahpohrteh?
We're in a terrible hurry___	Llevamos mucha prisa
	lyehbahmohs moochah preesah
Could you forward_____ my mail to this address?	¿Podría enviarme la correspondencia a esta dirección?
	pohdreeah ehnbyahrmeh lah kohrrehspohndehnthyah ah ehstah deerehkthyohn?
Could we leave our_____ luggage here until we leave?	¿Podríamos dejar las maletas aquí hasta que nos marchemos?
	pohdreeahmohs deh__h__ahr lahs mahlehtahs ahkee ahstah keh nohs mahrchehmohs?
Thanks for your _____ hospitality	Muchas gracias por la hospitalidad
	moochahs grahthyahs pohr lah ohspeetahleedahdh

Money matters

Money matters

● **In general,** banks are open to the public between 9am and 2pm; they are closed on Saturdays. In large cities it is possible to find main branches open until 4.30. To exchange currency a passport is required. Some travel agencies also provide facilities. The sign *cambio* indicates that money can be exchanged. Hotels may also offer this service, but at a less favourable rate.

8.1 **B**anks

Where can I find a_____ bank/an exchange office around here?	¿Dónde hay un banco/una oficina de cambios por aquí? *dohndeh ay oon bahnkoh/oonah ohfeetheenah deh kahmbyohs pohr ahkee?*
Where can I cash this_____ traveller's cheque/giro cheque?	¿Dónde puedo cambiar este cheque de viajero/este cheque postal? *dohndeh pwehdoh kahmbyahr ehsteh chehkeh deh byah<u>h</u>ehroh/ehsteh chehkeh pohstahl?*
Can I cash this...here? _____	¿Puedo cambiar aquí este...? *pwehdoh kahmbyahr ahkee ehsteh...?*
Can I withdraw money_____ on my credit card here?	¿Se puede sacar dinero con una tarjeta de crédito? *seh pwehdeh sahkahr deenehroh kohn oonah tahr<u>h</u>ehtah deh krehdeetoh?*
What's the minimum/_____ maximum amount?	¿Cuál es el mínimo/el máximo? *kwahl ehs ehl meeneemoh/ehl mahxeemoh?*
Can I take out less_____ than that?	¿También puedo sacar menos? *tahmbyehn pwehdoh sahkahr mehnohs?*
I've had some money_____ transferred here. Has it arrived yet?	He pedido un giro telegráfico. ¿Me ha llegado ya? *eh pehdeedoh oon <u>h</u>eeroh tehlehgrahfeekoh. meh ah lyehgahdoh yah?*
These are the details _____ of my bank in the UK	Estos son los datos de mi banco en el Reino Unido *ehstohs sohn lohs dahtohs deh mee bahnkoh ehn ehl reynoh ooneedoh*
This is my bank/giro_____ number	Este es mi número de cuenta bancaria/de la caja postal *ehsteh ehs mee noomehroh deh kwehntah bahnkahryah/deh lah kah<u>h</u>ah pohstahl*
I'd like to change _____ some money	Quisiera cambiar dinero *keesyehrah kahmbyahr deenehroh*
– pounds into... _____	Libras esterlinas por... *leebrahs ehstehrleenahs pohr...*
– dollars into... _____	Dólares estadounidenses por... *dohlahrehs ehstahdohooneedehnsehs pohr...*
What's the exchange _____ rate?	¿A cuánto está el cambio? *ah kwahntoh ehstah ehl kahmbyoh?*
Could you give me _____ some small change with it?	¿Me podría dar sencillo/cambio? *meh pohdreeah dahr sehntheelyoh/kahmbyoh?*
This is not right _____	Esto está mal *ehstoh ehstah mahl*

75

Firme aquí _____	Sign here, please
Tiene que rellenar esto _____	Fill this out, please
¿Me permite su pasaporte? _____	Could I see your passport, please?
¿Me permite su carnet de identidad? ____	Could I see some identification, please?
¿Me permite su tarjeta de la _____ caja postal?	Could I see your girobank card, please?
¿Me permite su tarjeta del banco? _____	Could I see your bank card, please?

8 .2 Settling the bill

Could you put it on_____ my bill?	¿Podría cargarlo a mi cuenta? *pohdreeah kahrgahrloh ah mee kwehntah?*
Does this amount _____ include service?	¿Está incluido el servicio en esta cifra? *ehstah eenklooeedoh ehl sehrbeethyoh ehn ehstah theefrah?*
Can I pay by...?_____	¿Puedo pagar con...? *pwehdoh pahgahr kohn...?*
Can I pay by credit card?___	¿Puedo pagar con tarjeta de crédito? *pwehdoh pahgahr kohn tahr_hehtah deh krehdeetoh?*
Can I pay by traveller's ____ cheque?	¿Puedo pagar con un cheque de viajero? *pwehdoh pahgahr kohn oon chehkeh de byahhehroh?*
Can I pay with foreign _____ currency?	¿Puedo pagar con moneda extranjera? *pwehdoh pahgahr kohn mohnehdah ehxtrahn_hehrah?*
You've given me too _____ much/you haven't given me enough change	Me ha devuelto de más/de menos *meh ah dehbwehltoh deh mahs/deh mehnohs*
Could you check the_____ bill again, please?	¿Puede volver a hacer la cuenta? *pwehdeh bohlbehr ah ahtehhr lah kwehntah?*
Could I have a receipt, _____ please?	¿Podría darme un recibo? *pohdreeah dahrmeh oon rehtheeboh?*
I don't have enough _____ money on me	No me alcanza el dinero *noh meh ahlkahnthah ehl deenehroh*

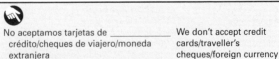

No aceptamos tarjetas de _____ crédito/cheques de viajero/moneda extranjera	We don't accept credit cards/traveller's cheques/foreign currency

This is for you _____	Tenga, esto es para usted *tehngah, ehstoh ehs pahrah oostehdh*
Keep the change _____	Quédese con la vuelta *kehdehseh kohn lah bwehltah*

Money matters 8

Post and telephone

9 Post and telephone

9.1 Post

For giros, see 8 Money matters

● **Post offices** are open from Monday to Saturday from 9am to 1 or 1.30pm. However stamps (*sellos*) can be bought at any *estanco* and many hotels also provide stamps. It is advisable to post letters at a post office, rather than the yellow mail boxes (*buzón*).

giros postales	telegramas	sellos
money orders	telegrams	stamps
paquetes		
parcels		

Where's...?	¿Dónde está...?
	dohndeh ehstah...?
Where's the post office?	¿Dónde hay una oficina de Correos por aquí?
	dohndeh ay oonah ohfeetheenah deh kohrrehohs pohr ahkee?
Where's the main post office?	¿Dónde está la oficina central de Correos?
	dohndeh ehstah lah ohfeetheenah thehntrahl deh kohrrehohs?
Where's the postbox?	¿Dónde hay un buzón por aquí?
	dohndeh ahee oon boothohn pohr ahkee?
Which counter should I go to...?	¿Cuál es la ventanilla para...?
	kwahl ehs lah behntahneelyah pahrah...?
– to send a fax	¿Cuál es la ventanilla para enviar un fax?
	kwahl ehs lah behntahneelyah pahrah ehnbyahr oon fahx?
– to change money	¿Cuál es la ventanilla para cambiar dinero?
	kwahl ehs lah behntahneelyah pahrah kahmbyahr deenehroh?
– to change giro cheques	¿Cuál es la ventanilla para los cheques postales?
	kwahl ehs lah behntahneelyah pahrah lohs chehkehs pohstahlehs?
– for a Telegraph Money Order?	¿Cuál es la ventanilla para los giros telegráficos?
	kwahl ehs lah behntahneelyah pahrah lohs heerohs tehlehgrahfeekohs?
Poste restante	Lista de correos
	leestah deh kohrrehohs
Is there any mail for me?My name's...	¿Hay carta para mí? Me llamo...
	ay kahrtah pahrah mee? meh lyahmoh...

Stamps

What's the postage _____ for a...to...?	¿Cuánto se le pone a un(a)...para...? *kwahntoh seh leh pohneh ah oon(ah)...pahrah...?*
Are there enough _____ stamps on it?	¿Lleva suficiente franqueo? *lyehbah soofeethyehnteh frahnkehoh?*
I'd like... ...peseta stamps __	Déme...sellos de... *dehmeh...sehlyohs deh...*
I'd like to send this... _____	Quisiera enviar esto... *keesyehrah ehnbyahr ehstoh...*
– express _____	Quisiera enviar esto por correo urgente *keesyehrah ehnbyahr ehstoh pohr kohrrehoh oorhehnteh*
– by air mail _____	Quisiera enviar esto por avión *keesyehrah ehnbyahr ehstoh pohr ahbyohn*
– by registered mail _____	Quisiera enviar esto certificado *keesyehrah ehnbyahr ehstoh thehrteefeekahdoh*

Telegram / fax

I'd like to send a _____ telegram to...	Quisiera mandar un telegrama a... *keesyehrah mahndahr oon tehlehgrahmah ah...*
How much is that _____ per word?	¿Cuánto cuesta por palabra? *kwahntoh kwehstah pohr pahlahbrah?*
This is the text I want_____ to send	Este es el texto que quiero enviar *ehsteh ehs ehl tehxtoh keh kyehroh ehnbyahr*
Shall I fill in the form _____ myself?	¿Relleno yo mismo el formulario? *rehlyehnoh yoh meesmoh ehl fohrmoolahryoh?*
Can I make photocopies/___ send a fax here?	¿Se pueden hacer fotocopias/se puede enviar un fax aquí? *seh pwehdehn ahtehr fohtohkohpyahs/seh pwehdeh ehnbyahr oon fahx ahkee?*
How much is it_____ per page?	¿Cuánto cuesta por página? *kwahntoh kwehstah pohr pahheenah?*

.2 Telephone

See also 1.8 Telephone alphabet

● **All phone booths** offer a direct international service to the UK or US (07 - country code 44 (UK) or 1 (US) – trunk code minus 0 – number). Area codes are displayed. It is easier, and may even be cheaper to place your call from the *Telefónica* or telephone office. When phoning someone in Spain, you will not be greeted with the subscriber's name but *diga* or *dígame*.

Is there a phone box _____ around here?	¿Hay alguna cabina telefónica por aquí? *ay ahlgoonah kahbeenah tehlehfohneekah pohr ahkee?*
Could I use your _____ phone, please?	¿Podría usar su teléfono? *pohdreeah oosahr soo tehlehfohnoh?*

Do you have a _____ (city/region)...phone directory?	¿Tiene una guía de teléfonos de la ciudad/la provincia de...?
	tyehneh oonah gheeah deh tehlehfohnohs deh lah thyoodahdh/lah prohbeenthyah deh...?
Where can I get a _____ phone card?	¿Dónde puedo conseguir una tarjeta de teléfonos?
	dohndeh pwehdoh kohnsehgheer oonah tarrhehtah deh tehlehfohnohs?
Could you give me...? _____	¿Me podría dar...?
	meh pohdreeah dahr...?
– the number for _____ international directory enquiries	¿Me podría dar el número de información internacional?
	meh pohdreeah dahr ehl noomehroh deh eenfohrmahthyohn eentehrnahthyohnahl?
– the number of room... ___	¿Me podría dar el número de la habitación...?
	meh pohdreeah dahr ehl noomehroh deh lah ahbeetahthyohn...?
– the international _____ access code	¿Me podría dar el indicativo internacional?
	meh pohdreeah dahr ehl eendeekahteeboh eentehrnahthyonahl...?
– the country code for...____	¿Me podría dar el indicativo de...?
	meh pohdreeah dahr ehl eendeekahteeboh deh...?
– the trunk code for... _____	¿Me podría dar el prefijo de...?
	meh pohdreeah dahr ehl prehfeehoh deh...?
– the number of... _____	¿Me podría dar el número de abonado de...?
	meh pohdreeah dahr ehl noomehroh deh ahbohnahdoh deh...?
Could you check if this ____ number's correct?	¿Podría controlar si está bien este número?
	pohdreeah kohntrohlahr see ehstah byehn ehsteh noomehroh?
Can I dial international_____ direct?	¿Se puede llamar directamente al extranjero?
	seh pwehdeh lyahmahr deerehktahmehnteh ahl ehxtrahnhehroh?
Do I have to go through ___ the switchboard?	¿Hay que llamar por operadora?
	ay keh lyahmahr pohr ohpehrahdohrah?
Do I have to dial '0'_____ first?	¿Hay que marcar primero el cero?
	ay keh mahrkahr preemehroh ehl thehroh?
Do I have to book _____ my calls?	¿Hay que pedir línea?
	ay keh pehdeer leenehah?
Could you dial this _____ number for me, please?	¿Podría usted llamar a este número?
	pohdreeah oostehdh lyahmahr ah ehsteh noomehroh?
Could you put me _____ through to.../extension..., please?	¿Me podría poner con.../con la extensión...?
	meh pohdreeah pohnehr kohn.../kohn lah ehxtehnsyohn...?
I'd like to place a _____ reverse-charge call to...	Quisiera una llamada de cobro revertido a...
	keesyehrah oonah lyahmahdah deh kohbroh rehbehrteedoh ah...

What's the charge per minute?	¿Cuánto cuesta por minuto?
	kwahntoh kwehstah pohr meenootoh?
Have there been any calls for me?	¿Ha habido alguna llamada para mí?
	ah ahbeedoh ahlgoonah lyahmahdah pahrah mee?

The conversation

Hello, this is... _____	Buenos días, soy...
	bwehnohs deeahs, soy...
Who is this, please? _____	¿Con quién hablo?
	kohn kyehn ahbloh?
Is this...? _____	¿Hablo con...?
	ahbloh kohn...?
I'm sorry, I've dialled the wrong number	Perdone, me he equivocado de número
	pehrdohneh, meh eh ehkeebohkahdoh deh noomehroh
I can't hear you _____	No le oigo bien
	noh leh oygoh byehn
I'd like to speak to... _____	Quisiera hablar con...
	keesyehrah ahblahr kohn...
Is there anybody who speaks English?	¿Hay alguien que hable inglés?
	ay ahlghyehn keh ahbleh eenglehs?
Extension..., please _____	¿Me pone con la extensión...?
	meh pohneh kohn lah ehxtehnsyohn...?
Could you ask him/her to call me back?	¿Podría decirle que me llame?
	pohdreeah dehtheerleh keh meh lyahmeh?
My name's... _____ My number's...	Me llamo...Mi número es...
	meh lyahmoh...mee noomehroh ehs...
Could you tell him/her I called?	¿Puede decirle que he llamado?
	pwehdeh dehtheerleh keh eh lyahmahdoh?
I'll call back tomorrow _____	Lo/la volveré a llamar mañana
	loh/lah bohlbehreh ah lyahmahr mahnyahnah

Post and telephone

Lo llaman por teléfono _____	There's a phone call for you
Primero tiene que marcar el cero _____	You have to dial '0' first
Un momento, por favor _____	One moment, please
No contestan _____	There's no answer
Está comunicando _____	The line's engaged
¿Quiere esperar? _____	Do you want to hold?
Ahora le paso _____	Putting you through
Se ha equivocado de número _____	You've got a wrong number
El señor/la señora...no está en estos momentos.	He's/she's not here right now
El señor/la señora...no estará hasta... _____	He'll/she'll be back...
Este es el contestador automático de...	This is the answering machine of...

Shopping

Shopping

● **Opening times:** Monday to Friday, 9.30am-1.30pm and 5pm-8pm.
Department stores are open in the afternoons from 4pm and remain
open on Saturdays. Other shops generally close on Saturdays at 1pm.
In tourist areas shops open for longer periods.
Chemists display the list of *farmacias de guardia* (those open on
Sundays and after hours).

almacén
department store

antigüedades
antiques

artículos de deporte
sports shop

artículos del hogar
household goods

artículos dietéticos
health food shop

artículos fotográficos
camera shop

artículos usados
second hand goods

autoservicio
self service

bicicletas
bicycle shop

bodega
off licence

bricolaje
DIY-store

carnicería
butcher's shop

casa de música
music shop

centro comercial
shopping centre

comestibles
grocery store

decoración
  (de interiores)
interior design shop

droguería
household products
  and cosmetics

electrodomésticos
electrical appliances

estanco
tobacconist

farmacia
chemist

ferretería
hardware shop

floristería
florist

frutas y verduras
greengrocer

galería comercial
shopping arcade

heladería
ice cream parlour

joyería
jeweller

juguetería
toy shop

lavandería
laundry

lechería
dairy

librería
book shop

mercado
market

mercería
draper

óptica
optician

panadería
bakery

pastelería
cake shop

peluquería (señoras,
  caballeros)
hairdresser

perfumería
cosmetics

pescadería
fishmonger

quiosco
news stand

recuerdos de viaje
souvenir shop

reparación de
  bicicletas
bicycle repair shop

revistas y prensa
newsagent

salón de belleza
beauty parlour

supermercado
supermarket

tienda
shop

tienda de modas
clothes shop

tintorería
drycleaner

zapatería
shoe shop

zapatero
cobbler

Shopping

Where can I get...?	¿Dónde puedo conseguir...?
	dohndeh pwehdoh kohnsehgheer...?
When does this shop open?	¿De qué hora a qué hora abren?
	deh keh ohrah ah keh ohrah ahbrehn?
Could you tell me where the...department is?	¿Me podría indicar la sección de...?
	meh pohdreeah eendeekahr lah sehkthyohn deh...?
Could you help me, please? I'm looking for...	¿Podría ayudarme? Busco...
	pohdreeah ahyoodahrmeh? booskoh...
Do you sell British/American newspapers?	¿Venden periódicos británicos/americanos?
	behndehn pehryohdeekohs breetahneekohs/ahmehreekahnohs?

¿Lo/la atienden? _____ Are you being served?

No, I'd like...	No. Quisiera...
	noh. keesyehrah...
I'm just looking, if that's all right	Sólo estoy mirando, gracias
	sohloh ehstoy meerahndoh, grahthyahs

¿Algo más? _____ Anything else?

Yes, I'd also like...	Sí, también déme...
	see, tahmbyehn dehmeh...
No, thank you. That's all	No, gracias. Es todo
	noh, grahthyahs, ehs tohdoh
Could you show me...?	¿Me podría mostrar...?
	meh pohdreeah mohstrahr...?
I'd prefer...	Prefiero...
	prehfyehroh...
This is not what I'm looking for	No es lo que busco
	noh ehs loh keh booskoh
Thank you. I'll keep looking	Gracias. Voy a seguir mirando
	grahthyahs. boy ah sehgheer meerahndoh
Do you have something...?	¿No tendría algo ...?
	noh tehndreeah ahlgoh ...?
– less expensive?	¿No tendría algo más barato?
	noh tehndreeah ahlgoh mahs bahrahtoh?
– smaller?	¿No tendría algo más pequeño?
	noh tehndreeah ahlgoh mahs pehkehnyoh?
– larger?	¿No tendría algo más grande?
	noh tehndreeah ahlgoh mahs grahndeh?
I'll take this one	Me llevo éste/ésta
	meh lyehboh ehsteh/ehstah
Does it come with instructions?	¿Viene con instrucciones?
	byehneh kohn eenstrookthyohnehs?
It's too expensive	Me parece muy caro
	meh pahrehtheh mwee kahroh

Shopping

I'll give you... _____	Le doy... *leh doy...*
Could you keep this for ____ me? I'll come back for it later	¿Me lo/la podría guardar? Volveré más tarde a buscarlo *meh loh/lah pohdreeah gwahrdahr?* *bohlbehreh mahs tahrdeh ah booskahrloh*
Have you got a bag _____ for me, please?	¿Tendría una bolsita? *tehndreeah oonah bohlseetah?*
Could you giftwrap _____ it, please?	¿Me lo podría envolver para regalo? *meh loh pohdreeah ehnbohlbehr pahrah rehgahloh?*

Lo siento; no lo tenemos _____	I'm sorry, we don't have that
Lo siento; ya no queda _____	I'm sorry, we're sold out
Lo siento, hasta el...no lo _____ tendremos	I'm sorry, that won't be in until...
Pague en la caja, por favor _____	You can pay at the cash desk
No aceptamos tarjetas de crédito _____	We don't accept credit cards
No aceptamos cheques de viajero _____	We don't accept traveller's cheques
No aceptamos moneda extranjera _____	We don't accept foreign currency

10 .2 Food

I'd like a hundred _____ grams of..., please	Quisiera cien gramos de... *keesyehrah thyehn grahmohs deh...*
– half a kilo of... _____	Quisiera medio kilo de... *keesyehrah mehdyoh keeloh deh...*
– a kilo of... _____	Quisiera un kilo de... *keesyehrah oon keeloh deh...*
Could you...it for me, _____ please?	¿Me lo podría...? *meh loh pohdreeah...?*
Could you slice it/ _____ dice it for me, please?	¿Me lo podría cortar en lonchas/en trozos? *meh loh pohdreeah kohrtahr ehn lohnchahs/ehn trohthohs?*
Could you grate it _____ for me, please?	¿Me lo podría rallar? *meh loh pohdreeah rahlyahr?*
Can I order it? _____	¿Se lo podría encargar? *seh loh pohdreeah ehnkahrgahr?*
I'll pick it up tomorrow/ ____ at...	Pasaré a buscarlo mañana/a las... *pahsahreh ah booskahrloh mahnyahnah/ah lahs...*
Can you eat/drink this? ____	¿Es para comer/beber? *ehs pahrah kohmehr/behbehr?*
What's in it? _____	¿Qué lleva dentro? *keh lyehbah dehntroh?*

I saw something in the ____ window. Shall I point it out? | He visto algo en el escaparate. ¿Se lo enseño?
eh beestoh ahlgoh ehn ehl ehskahpahrahteh, seh loh ehnsehnyoh?

I'd like something to_____ go with this | Busco algo que haga juego con esto
booskoh ahlgoh keh ahgah hwehgoh kohn ehstoh

Do you have shoes_____ in this colour? | ¿Tiene zapatos de este color?
tyehneh thahpahtohs deh ehsteh kohlohr?

I'm a size...in the UK_____ | En el Reino Unido tengo el número...
ehn ehl reheenoh ooneedoh tehngoh ehl noomehroh...

Can I try this on? _____ | ¿Me lo podría probar?
meh loh pohdreeah prohbahr?

Where's the fitting_____ room? | ¿Dónde está el probador?
dohndeh ehstah ehl prohbahdohr?

It doesn't fit_____ | No me vale
noh meh bahleh

This is the right size _____ | Este es mi número
ehsteh ehs mee noomehroh

It doesn't suit me_____ | No me está bien
noh meh ehstah byehn

Do you have this/ _____ these in...? | ¿Tiene éste/ésta, pero en...?
tyehneh ehsteh/ehstah pehroh ehn...?

The heel's too high/low ____ | El tacón me parece muy alto/bajo
ehl tahkohn meh pahrehtheh mwee ahltoh/bahhoh

Is this/are these _____ genuine leather? | ¿Es/son de piel auténtica?
ehs/sohn deh pyehl ah-ootehnteekah?

I'm looking for a..._____ for a...-year-old baby/child | Busco un/una...para un bebé/niño de...años
booskoh oon/oonah...pahrah oon behbeh/neenyoh deh...ahnyohs

I'd like a... ... _____ | Quisiera un/una...de...
keesyehrah oon/oonah...deh...

– silk _____ | Quisiera un/una...de seda
keesyehrah oon/oonah...deh sehdah

– cotton _____ | Quisiera un/una...de algodón
keesyehrah oon/oonah...deh ahlgohdohn

– woollen _____ | Quisiera un/una...de lana
keesyehrah oon/oonah...deh lahnah

– linen_____ | Quisiera un/una...de hilo
keesyehrah oon/oonah...deh eeloh

What temperature_____ can I wash it at? | ¿A qué temperatura lo puedo lavar?
ah keh tehmpehrahtoorah loh pwehdoh lahbahr?

Will it shrink in the _____ wash? | ¿Encoge al lavarlo?
enkohheh ahl lahbahrloh?

No planchar	Colgar mojado	Lavado a mano
Do not iron	Drip dry	Hand wash
No centrifugar	Lavado en seco	Lavado a máquina
Do not spin dry	Dry clean	Machine wash

At the cobbler

Could you mend _____ these shoes?	¿Podría arreglar estos zapatos? *pohdreeah ahrrehglahr ehstohs thahpahtohs?*
Could you put new _____ soles/heels on these?	¿Podría ponerle nuevas suelas/nuevos tacones? *pohdreeah pohnehrleh nwehbahs swehlahs/nwehbohs tahkohnehs?*
When will they be _____ ready?	¿Para cuándo van a estar? *pahrah kwahndoh bahn ah ehstahr?*
I'd like..., please _____	Quisiera..., por favor *keesyehrah..., pohr fahbohr*
– a tin of shoe polish _____	Quisiera una crema para zapatos *keesyehrah oonah krehmah pahrah thahpahtohs*
– a pair of shoelaces_____	Quisiera un par de cordones *keesyehrah oon pahr deh kohrdohnehs*

🔟 .4 Photographs and video

I'd like a film for this_____ camera, please	Quisiera un rollo/carrete para esta cámara *keesyehrah oon rohlyoh/kahrrehteh pahrah ehstah kahmahrah*
– a 126 cartridge _____	Quisiera una película en cassette de 126 *keesyehrah oonah pehleekoolah ehn kahseht deh thyehntoh beheenteesehees*
– a 35mm colour slide _____	Un carrete de 35mm para diapositivas en color *oon kahrrehteh deh treyntah ee theenkoh meeleemehtrohs pahrah deeapohseeteebahs ehn kohlohr*
– a 35mm colour _____ print	Un carrete de 35mm en color *oon kahrrehteh deh treyntah ee theenkoh meeleemehtrohs ehn kohlohr*
– a 35mm black _____ and white	Un carrete de 35mm en blanco y negro *oon kahrrehteh deh treyntah ee theenkoh meeleemehtrohs ehn blahnkoh ee nehgroh*
– a videotape _____	Quisiera una cinta de vídeo *keesyehrah oonah theentah deh veedehoh*
colour/black and white_____	color/blanco y negro *kohlohr/blahnkoh ee nehgroh*
super eight _____	superocho *soopehrohchoh*
12/24/36 exposures _____	doce/veinticuatro/treinta y seis fotos *dohtheh/beheenteekwahtroh/treheentah ee sehees fohtohs*
ASA/DIN number_____	valor ISO *bahlohr eesoh*
daylight film _____	película para luz natural *pehleekoolah pahrah looth nahtoorahl*
film for artificial light _____	película para luz artificial *pehleekoolah pahrah looth ahrteefeethyahl*

Problems

Could you load the _____
film for me, please?
¿Me podría poner el rollo/carrete en la
cámara?
*meh pohdreeah pohnehr ehl
rohlyoh/kahrrehteh ehn lah kahmahrah?*

Could you take the film ____
out for me, please?
¿Me podría sacar el rollo/carrete de la
cámara?
*meh pohdreeah sahkahr ehl
rohlyoh/kahrrehteh deh lah kahmahrah?*

Should I replace_____
the batteries?
¿Tengo que cambiar las pilas?
tehngoh keh kahmbyahr lahs peelahs?

Could you have a look ____
at my camera, please?
It's not working
¿Me podría revisar la cámara? Ya no
funciona
*meh pohdreeah rehbeesahr lah kahmahrah?
yah noh foonthyohnah*

The...is broken _____
Está estropeado el...
ehstah ehstrohpehahdoh ehl...

The film's jammed _____
Se ha atascado el rollo/carrete
*seh ah ahtahskahdoh ehl rohlyoh
/kahrrehteh*

The film's broken_____
Se ha roto el rollo/carrete
seh ah rohtoh ehl rohlyoh/kahrrehteh

The flash isn't working ____
No funciona el flash
noh foonthyohnah ehl flahsh

Processing and prints

I'd like to have this film ____
developed/printed,
please
Quisiera mandar a revelar/copiar este
rollo/carrete
*keesyehrah mahndahr ah
rehbehlahr/kohpyahr ehsteh
rohlyoh/kahrrehteh*

I'd like...prints from_____
each negative
Quisiera...copias de cada negativo
*keesyehrah...kohpyahs deh kahdah
nehgahteeboh*

glossy/mat_____
brillante/mate
breelyahnte/mahteh

I'd like to reorder_____
these photos
Quisiera encargar más copias de
estas fotos
*keesyehrah ehnkahrgahr mahs kohpyahs deh
ehstahs fohtohs*

I'd like to have this _____
photo enlarged
Quisiera una ampliación de esta foto
*keesyehrah oonah ahmplyahthyohn deh
ehstah fohtoh*

How much is_____
processing?
¿Cuánto sale el revelado?
kwahntoh sahleh ehl rehbehlahdoh?

– printing? _____
¿Cuánto sale el copiado?
kwahntoh sahleh ehl kohpyahdoh?

– extra copies? _____
¿Cuánto salen las copias adicionales?
*kwahntoh sahlehn lahs kohpyahs
ahdeethyohnahlehs?*

– the enlargement? _____
¿Cuánto sale la ampliación?
kwahntoh sahleh lah ahmplyahthyohn?

When will they_____
be ready?
¿Para cuándo van a estar?
pahrah kwahndoh bahn ah ehstahr?

Do I have to make an _____ appointment?	¿Tengo que pedir hora? *tehngoh keh pehdeer ohrah?*
Can I come in straight _____ away?	¿Podría atenderme en seguida? *pohdreeah ahtehndehrmeh ehn sehgheedah?*
How long will I have_____ to wait?	¿Cuánto tengo que esperar? *kwahntoh tehngoh keh ehspehrahr?*
I'd like a shampoo/ _____ haircut	Quisiera lavarme/cortarme el pelo *keesyehrah lahbahrmeh/kohrtahrmeh ehl pehloh*
I'd like a shampoo for _____ oily/dry hair, please	Quisiera un champú para cabello graso/seco *keesyehrah oon chahmpoo pahrah kahbehlyoh grahsoh/sehkoh*
an anti-dandruff_____ shampoo	Quisiera un champú anticaspa *keesyehrah oon chahmpoo ahnteekahspah*
– a shampoo for_____ permed/coloured hair	Quisiera un champú para cabello con permanente/teñido. *keesyehrah oon chahmpoo pahrah kahbehlyoh kohn pehrmahnehnteh/tehnyeedoh*
– a colour rinse shampoo __	Quisiera un champú color *keesyehrah oon chahmpoo kohlohr*
– a shampoo with _____ conditioner	Quisiera un champú con acondicionador *keesyehrah oon chahmpoo kohn ahkohndeethyohnahdohr*
– highlights _____	Quisiera que me hagan claritos *keesyehrah keh meh ahgahn klahreetohs*
Do you have a colour_____ chart, please?	¿Tendría una carta de colores? *tehndreeah oonah kahrtah deh kohlohrehs?*
I want to keep it the _____ same colour	Quiero conservar el mismo color *kyehroh kohnsehrbahr ehl meesmoh kohlohr*
I'd like it darker/lighter_____	Quisiera un color más oscuro/más claro *keesyehrah oon kohlohr mahs ohskooroh/mahs klahroh*
I'd like/I don't want _____ hairspray	(No) quiero fijador *(noh) kyehroh feehahdohr*
– gel_____	(No) quiero gel *(noh) kyehroh hehl*
– lotion _____	(No) quiero loción *(noh) kyehroh lohthyohn*
I'd like a short fringe _____	Quisiera el flequillo corto *keesyehrah ehl flehkeelyoh kohrtoh*
Not too short at _____ the back	No lo quisiera demasiado corto por detrás *noh loh keesyehrah dehmahsyahdoh kohrtoh pohr dehtrahs*
Not too long here _____	No lo quisiera demasiado largo aquí *noh loh keesyehrah dehmahsyahdoh lahrgoh ahkee*
I'd like/I don't want _____ (many) curls	(No) quisiera (demasiados) rizos *(noh) keesyehrah (dehmahsyadohs) reethohs*

Shopping

10

It needs a little/_____ a lot taken off	Hay que cortar sólo un trocito/un buen trozo *ay keh kohrtahr sohloh oon trohtheetoh/oon bwehn trohthoh*
I want a completely _____ different style	Quisiera un modelo totalmente diferente *keesyehrah oon mohdehloh tohtahlmehnteh deefehrehnteh*
I'd like it the same as... ____	Quisiera el pelo como... *keesyehrah ehl pehloh kohmoh...*
– as that lady's _____	Quisiera el pelo como esa señora *keesyehrah ehl pehloh kohmoh ehsah sehnyohrah*
– as in this photo_____	Quisiera el pelo como en esta foto *keesyehrah ehl pehloh kohmoh ehn ehstah fohtoh*
Could you put the _____ drier up/down a bit?	¿Podría poner el casco más alto/bajo? *pohdreeah pohnehr ehl kahskoh mahs ahltoh/ bahhoh?*
I'd like a facial_____	Quisiera una máscara facial *keesyehrah oonah mahskahrah fahthyahl*
– a manicure _____	Quisiera que me hagan manicura *keesyehrah keh meh ahgahn mahneekoorah*
– a massage _____	Quisiera que me hagan masaje *keesyehrah keh meh ahgahn mahsahheh*
Could you trim _____ my fringe?	¿Me podría recortar el flequillo? *meh pohdreeah rehkohrtahr ehl flehkeelyoh?*
– my beard? _____	¿Me podría recortar la barba? *meh pohdreeah rehkohrtahr lah bahrbah?*
– my moustache? _____	¿Me podría recortar el bigote? *meh pohdreeah rehkohrtahr ehl beegohteh?*
I'd like a shave, please____	Aféiteme, por favor *ahfeheetehmeh, pohr fahbohr*
I'd like a wet shave, _____ please	Aféiteme a navaja, por favor *ahfeheetehmeh ah nahbahhah, pohr fahbohr*

¿Cómo quiere el corte de pelo? _____	How do you want it cut?
¿Qué modelo deseaba? _____	What style did you have in mind?
¿Qué color quiere?_____	What colour do you want it?
¿Esta temperatura le va bien?_____	Is the temperature all right for you?
¿Quiere algo para leer?_____	Would you like something to read?
¿Quiere algo para beber?_____	Would you like a drink?
¿Así está bien? _____	Is this what you had in mind?

Shopping

10

At the Tourist Information Centre

11 **A**t the Tourist Information Centre

11 .1 **P**laces of interest

At the Tourist Information Centre

Where's the Tourist _____ Information, please?
¿Dónde está la oficina de turismo?
dohndeh ehstah lah ohfeetheenah deh tooreesmoh?

Do you have a city map?___
¿Tendría un plano de la ciudad?
tehndreeah oon plahnoh deh lah thyoodahdh?

Where is the museum? ____
¿Dónde está el museo?
dohndeh ehstah ehl moosehoh?

Where can I find _____ a church?
¿Dónde podría encontrar una iglesia?
dohndeh pohdreeah ehnkohntrahr oonah eeglehsyah?

Could you give me _____ some information about...?
¿Me podría dar información sobre...?
meh pohdreeah dahr eenfohrmahthyohn sohbreh...?

How much is that? _____
¿Cuánto le debemos por esto?
kwahntoh leh dehbehmohs pohr ehstoh?

What are the main _____ places of interest?
¿Cuáles son los sitios más interesantes para visitar?
kwahlehs sohn lohs seetyohs mahs eentehrehsahntehs pahrah veeseetahr?

Could you point them ____ out on the map?
¿Me los podría señalar en el plano?
meh lohs pohdreeah sehnyahlahr ehn ehl plahnoh?

What do you _____ recommend?
¿Qué nos recomienda?
keh nohs rehkohmyehndah?

We'll be here for a_____ few hours
Pensamos quedarnos unas horas
pehnsahmohs kehdahrnohs oonahs ohrahs

– a day _____
Pensamos quedarnos un día
pehnsahmohs kehdahrnohs oon deeah

– a week_____
Pensamos quedarnos una semana
pehnsahmohs kehdahrnohs oonah sehmahnah

We're interested in... _____
Nos interesa...
nohs eentehrehsah...

Is there a scenic walk_____ around the city?
¿Hay algún circuito turístico para visitar la ciudad a pie?
ay ahlgoon theerkweetoh tooreesteekoh pahrah veeseetar lah thyoodahdh ah pyeh?

How long does it take? ____
¿Cuánto dura?
kwahntoh doorah?

Where does it start/end? ___
¿De dónde sale?/¿Dónde termina?
deh dohndeh sahleh?/dohndeh tehrmeenah?

Are there any boat _____ cruises here?
¿Hay excursiones en barco?
ay ehxkoorsyohnehs ehn bahrkoh?

Where can we board? ____
¿Dónde se puede embarcar?
dohndeh seh pwehdeh ehmbahrkahr?

Are there any bus tours?___
¿Hay excursiones en autocar?
ay ehxkoorsyohnehs ehn ahootohkahr?

Where do we get on?_____
¿De dónde salen?
deh dohndeh sahlehn?

Is there a guide who_____ speaks English?
¿Hay algún guía que hable inglés?
ay ahlgoon gheeah keh ahbleh eenglehs?

What trips can we take ____ around the area?	¿Qué excursiones se pueden hacer en los alrededores?
	keh ehxkoorsyohnehs seh pwehdehn ahthehr ehn lohs ahlrehdehdohrehs?
Are there any _____ excursions?	¿Hay excursiones organizadas?
	ay ehxkoorsyohnehs ohrgahneethahdahs?
Where do they go to? ____	¿Hacia dónde van?
	ahthyah dohndeh bahn?
We'd like to go to..._____	Quisiéramos ir a...
	keesyehrahmohs eer ah...
How long is the trip? _____	¿Cuánto se tarda en llegar?
	kwahntoh seh tahrdah ehn lyehgahr?
How long do we _____ stay in...?	¿Cuánto dura la visita a...?
	kwahntoh doorah lah beeseetah ah...
Are there any guided _____ tours?	¿Hay visitas guiadas?
	ay beeseetahs gheeahdahs?
How much free time_____ will we have there?	¿Cuánto tiempo libre tenemos allí?
	kwahntoh tyehmpoh leebreh tehnehmohs alyee?
We want to go hiking_____	Nos gustaría hacer una excursión a pie
	nohs goostahreeah ahtehr oonah ehxkoorsyohn ah pyeh
Can we hire a guide? _____	¿Es posible contratar un guía?
	ehs pohseebleh kohntrahtahr oon gheeah?
Can I book mountain _____ huts?	¿Se puede hacer una reserva para un refugio (en la montaña)?
	seh pwehdeh ahtehr oonah rehsehrbah pahrah oon rehfoohyoh (ehn lah mohntahnyah)?
What time does... _____ open/close?	¿A qué hora abre/cierra...?
	ah keh ohrah ahbreh/thyehrrah...?
What days is...open/_____ closed?	¿Qué días tiene abierto/cerrado...?
	keh deeahs tyehneh ahbyehrtoh/thehrrahdoh...?
What's the admission_____ price?	¿Cuánto sale la entrada?
	kwahntoh sahleh lah ehntrahdah?
Is there a group _____ discount?	¿Hay descuento para grupos?
	ay dehskwehntoh pahrah groopohs?
Is there a child _____ discount?	¿Hay descuento para niños?
	ay dehskwehntoh pahrah neenyohs?
Is there a discount_____ for pensioners?	¿Hay descuento para jubilados?
	ay dehskwehntoh pahrah hoobeelahdohs?
Can I take (flash) _____ photos/can I film here?	¿Se pueden sacar fotos (con flash)/ filmar aquí?
	seh pwehdehn sahkahr fohtohs(kohn flahsh)/feelmahr ahkee?
Do you have any _____ postcards of...?	¿Venden postales de...?
	behndehn pohstahlehs deh...?
Do you have an _____ English...?	¿Tiene un...en inglés?
	tyehneh oon...ehn eenglehs?
– an English catalogue?____	¿Tiene un catálogo en inglés?
	tyehneh oon kahtahlohgoh ehn eenglehs?
– an English programme?__	¿Tiene un programa en inglés?
	tyehneh oon prohgrahmah ehn eenglehs?
– an English brochure? ____	¿Tiene un folleto en inglés?
	tyehneh oon fohlyehtoh ehn eenglehs?

11

.2 Going out

● **At the cinema** most films are dubbed in Spanish. Sometimes there are only two showings, in the evening, at 7 and 11pm. In this case advance booking is advisable.

Do you have this _____ week's/month's entertainment guide?	¿Tiene la guía de los espectáculos de esta semana/este mes? *tyehneh lah gheeah deh lohs ehspehktahkoolohs deh ehstah sehmahnah/ehsteh mehs?*
What's on tonight? _____	¿Adónde podríamos ir esta noche? *ahdohndeh pohdreeahmohs eer ehstah nohcheh?*
We want to go to... _____	Nos gustaría ir a... *nohs goostahreeah eer ah...*
Which films are _____ showing?	¿Qué películas dan? *keh pehleekoolahs dahn?*
What sort of film is that?___	¿Qué clase de película es? *keh klahseh deh pehleekoolah ehs?*
suitable for everyone _____	para todos los públicos *pahrah tohdohs lohs poobleekohs*
not suitable for_____ children	prohibido para menores de 12/16 años *proheebeedoh pahrah mehnohrehs deh dohtheh/dyehtheesehees ahnyohs*
original version _____	versión original *behrsyohn ohreeheenahl*
subtitled _____	subtitulada *soobteetoolahdah*
dubbed _____	doblada *dohblahdah*
Is it a continuous_____ showing?	¿Es sesión continua? *ehs sehsyohn kohnteenooah?*
What's on at...? _____	¿Qué dan en...? *keh dahn ehn...?*
– the theatre? _____	¿Qué dan en el teatro? *keh dahn ehn ehl tehahtroh?*
– the concert hall?_____	¿Qué dan en la sala de conciertos? *keh dahn ehn lah sahlah deh kohnthyehrtohs?*
– the opera? _____	¿Qué dan en la ópera? *keh dahn ehn lah ohpehrah?*
Where can I find a good ___ disco around here?	¿Dónde hay una buena discoteca por aquí? *dohndeh ay oonah bwehnah deeskohtehkah pohr ahkee?*
Is it for members only? ____	¿Hay que ser socio? *ay keh sehr sohthyoh?*
Where can I find a good ___ cabaret club around here?	¿Dónde hay un buen cabaret por aquí? *dohndeh ay oon bwehn kahbahreh pohr ahkee?*
Is it evening wear only? ___	¿Hay que ir en traje de etiqueta? *ay keh eer ehn trahheh deh ehteekehtah?*

Should I/we dress up? _____	¿Es recomendable ir en traje de etiqueta?
	ehs rehkohmehndahbleh eer ehn trahheh
	deh ehteekehtah?
What time does the _____	¿A qué hora empieza el espectáculo?
show start?	*ah keh ohrah ehmpyehthah ehl*
	ehspehktahkooloh?
When's the next soccer _____	¿Cuándo es el próximo partido de fútbol?
match?	*kwahlndoh ehs ehl prohxeemoh pahrteedoh*
	deh footbohl?
Who's playing?_____	¿Quiénes juegan?
	kyehnehs hwehgahn?
I'd like an escort for _____	Quisiera contratar un/una acompañante
tonight. Could you	para esta noche. ¿Podría hacerme una
arrange that for me?	reserva?
	keesyehrah kohntrahtahr oon/oonah
	ahkohmpahnyahnteh pahrah ehstah
	nohcheh. podreeah ahtehrmeh oonah
	rehsehrbah?

🔟 .3 Booking tickets

Could you book some _____	¿Podría hacernos una reserva?
tickets for us?	*pohdreeah ahtehrnohs oonah rehsehrbah?*
We'd like to book... _____	Quisiéramos...entradas/una mesa...
tickets/a table...	*keesyehrahmohs...ehntrahdahs/oonah*
	mehsah...
– tickets/seats in the _____	Quisiéramos...entradas en la platea
stalls	*keesyehrahmohs...ehntrahdahs ehn lah*
	plahtehah
– tickets/seats on the _____	Quisiéramos...entradas en el palco
balcony	*keesyehrahmohs...ehntrahdahs ehn ehl*
	pahlkoh
– box seats _____	Quisiéramos...entradas en el palco
	privado
	keesyehrahmohs...ehntrahdahs ehn ehl
	pahlkoh preebahdoh
– a table at the front_____	Quisiéramos una mesa adelante
	keesyehrahmohs oonah mehsah
	ahdehlahnteh
– in the middle_____	Quisiéramos una mesa al centro
	keesyehrahmohs oonah mehsah ahl
	thehntroh
– at the back _____	Quisiéramos una mesa atrás
	keesyehrahmohs oonah mehsah ahtrahs
Could I book...seats for _____	¿Podría reservar...entradas para la función
the...o'clock	de las...?
performance?	*pohdreeah rehsehrbahr...ehntrahdahs pahrah*
	lah foonthyohn deh lahs...?
Are there any seats left _____	¿Quedan entradas para esta noche?
for tonight?	*kehdahn ehntrahdahs pahrah ehstah*
	nohcheh?
How much is a ticket? _____	¿Cuánto sale la entrada?
	kwahntoh sahleh lah ehntrahdah?

When can I pick the _____
tickets up?

¿Cuándo puedo pasar a retirar las
entradas?
*kwahndoh pwehdoh pahsahr ah rehteerahr
lahs ehntrahdahs?*

I've got a reservation _____

Tengo una reserva
tehngoh oonah rehsehrbah

My name's... _____

Me llamo...
meh lyahmoh...

🖐

¿Para qué función desea reservar? _____	Which performance do you want to book for?
¿Qué sector prefiere? _____	Where would you like to sit?
No hay billetes. _____	Everything's sold out
Sólo quedan entradas de pie _____	It's standing room only
Sólo quedan entradas en el palco _____	We've only got balcony seats left
Sólo quedan entradas en la galería _____	We've only got seats left in the gallery
Sólo quedan entradas en la platea _____	We've only got stalls seats left
Sólo quedan entradas adelante _____	We've only got seats left at the front
Sólo quedan entradas atrás _____	We've only got seats left at the back
¿Cuántas entradas quiere? _____	How many seats would you like?
Tiene que retirar las entradas antes de las... _____	You'll have to pick up the tickets before...o'clock
¿Me permite las entradas? _____	Tickets, please
Este es su asiento _____	This is your seat

11

Sports

12 .1 **S**porting questions

Where can we... _____ around here?	¿Dónde se puede...? *dohndeh seh pwehdeh...?*
Is there a... _____ around here?	¿Hay algún...por aquí cerca? *ay ahlgoon...pohr ahkee thehrkah?*
Can I hire a...here? _____	¿Alquilan...? *ahlkeelahn...?*
Can I take...lessons? _____	¿Dan clases de...? *dahn klahsehs deh...?*
How much is that per_____ hour/per day/class?	¿Cuánto sale por hora/día/clase? *kwahntoh sahleh pohr ohrah/deeah/klahseh?*
Do I need a permit _____ for that?	¿Se necesita un permiso? *seh nehthehseetah oon pehrmeesoh?*
Where can I get _____ the permit?	¿Dónde se consiguen los permisos? *dohndeh seh kohnseeghehn lohs pehrmeesohs?*

12 .2 **B**y the waterfront

Is it a long way to _____ the sea still?	¿Falta mucho para llegar al mar? *fahltah moochoh pahrah lyehgahr ahl mahr?*
Is there a...around here? ___	¿Hay algún...por aquí? *ay ahlgoon...pohr ahkee*
– an outdoor/indoor/_____ public swimming pool	¿Hay alguna piscina por aquí? *ay ahlgoonah peestheenah pohr ahkee?*
– a sandy beach _____	¿Hay alguna playa con arena por aquí? *ay ahlgoonah plahyah kohn ahrehnah pohr ahkee?*
– a nudist beach _____	¿Hay alguna playa nudista por aquí? *ay ahlgoonah plahyah noodeestah pohr ahkee?*
– mooring _____	¿Hay algún atracadero por aquí? *ay ahlgoon ahtrahkahdehroh pohr ahkee?*
Are there any rocks _____ here?	¿Hay rocas? *ay rohkahs?*
When's high/low tide? _____	¿Cuándo sube/baja la marea? *kwahndoh soobeh/bah__hah__ lah mahrehah?*
What's the water _____ temperature?	¿Qué temperatura tiene el agua? *keh tehmpehrahtoorah tyehneh ehl ahgwah?*
Is it (very) deep here? _____	¿Es (muy) profundo? *ehs mwee prohfoondoh?*
Can you stand here? _____	¿Se puede hacer pie? *seh pwehdeh ahtehr pyeh?*
Is it safe to swim here? ____	¿Es seguro para nadar? *ehs sehgooroh pahrah nahdahr?*
Are there any currents? ____	¿Hay corriente? *ay kohrryehnteh?*
Are there any rapids/ _____ waterfalls in this river?	¿Este río tiene rápidos/cascadas? *ehsteh reeoh tyehneh rahpeedohs/kahskahdahs?*
What does that flag/ _____ buoy mean?	¿Qué significa aquella bandera/boya? *keh seegneefeekah ahkehlyah bahndehrah/bohyah?*

Is there a life guard on duty here?	¿Hay algún vigilante de servicio?
	ay ahlgoon veeheelante deh sehrbeetheeoh?
Are dogs allowed here?	¿Está permitido traer perros?
	ehstah pehrmeeteedoh trahehr pehrrohs?
Is camping on the beach allowed?	¿Está permitido acampar en la playa?
	ehstah pehrmeeteedoh ahkahmpahr ehn lah plahyah?
Are we allowed to build a fire here?	¿Está permitido hacer fuego?
	ehstah pehrmeeteedoh ahthehr fwehgoh?

Peligro	Prohibido pescar	Prohibido bañarse
Danger	No fishing	No swimming
Aguas de pesca	Prohibido hacer	Permiso obligatorio
Fishing water	surfing	Permits only
	No surfing	

🔢 .3 In the snow

Can I take ski lessons here?	¿Dan clases de esquí?
	dahn klahsehs deh eskee?
for beginners/advanced	para principiantes/avanzados
	pahrah preentheepyahntehs/ahbahnthahdohs
How large are the groups?	¿De cuántas personas son los grupos?
	deh kwahntahs pehrsohnahs sohn lohs groopohs?
What language are the classes in?	¿En qué idioma son las clases?
	ehn keh eedyohmah sohn lahs klahsehs?
I'd like a lift pass, please	Quisiera un pase para las telesillas
	keesyehrah oon pahseh pahrah lahs tehlehseelyahs
Must I give you a passport photo?	¿Se necesita foto?
	seh nehthehseetah fohtoh?
Where can I have a passport photo taken?	¿Dónde puedo sacarme fotos?
	dohndeh pwehdoh sahkahrmeh fohtohs?
Where are the beginners' slopes?	¿Dónde están las pistas para principiantes?
	dohndeh ehstahn lahs peestahs pahrah preentheepyahntehs?
Are there any runs for cross-country skiing?	¿Hay pistas de esquí de fondo por aquí?
	ay peestahs deh ehskee deh fohndoh pohr ahkee?
Have the cross-country runs been marked?	¿Las pistas de esquí de fondo están señalizadas?
	lahs peestahs deh ehskee deh fohndoh ehstahn sehnyahleethahdahs?
Are the...in operation?	¿Están abiertos los...?
	ehstahn ahbyehrtohs lohs...?
– the ski lifts	¿Ya funcionan los telesquís?
	yah foonthyohnahn lohs tehlehskees?
– the chair lifts	¿Ya funcionan las telesillas?
	yah foonthyohnahn lahs tehlehseelyahs?
Are the slopes usable?	¿Están abiertas las pistas?
	ehstahn ahbyehrtahs lahs peestahs?

13

Sickness

13 **S**ickness

13.1 **C**all (fetch) the doctor

Could you call/fetch a_____ doctor quickly, please?
¿Podría llamar/ir a buscar rápido a un médico, por favor?
pohdreeah lyahmahr/eer ah booskahr rahpeedoh ah oon mehdeekoh, pohr fahbohr?

When does the doctor _____ have surgery?
¿Cuándo tiene consulta el médico?
kwahndoh tyehneh kohnsooltah ehl mehdeekoh?

When can the doctor _____ come?
¿Cuándo puede venir el médico?
kwahndoh pwehdeh behneer ehl mehdeekoh?

I'd like to make an_____ appointment to see the doctor
¿Podría pedirme hora con el médico?
pohdreeah pehdeermeh ohrah kohn ehl mehdeekoh?

I've got an appointment ___ to see the doctor at...
Tengo hora con el médico para las...
tehngoh ohrah kohn ehl mehdeekoh pahrah lahs...

Which doctor/chemist _____ has night/weekend duty?
¿Qué médico/farmacia está de guardia esta noche/este fin de semana?
keh mehdeekoh/fahrmahthyah ehstah deh gwahrdyah ehstah nohcheh/ehsteh feen deh sehmahnah?

13.2 **P**atient's ailments

I don't feel well _____
No me siento bien
noh meh syehntoh byehn

I'm dizzy_____
Tengo mareos
tehngoh mahrehohs

– ill_____
Estoy enfermo
ehstoy ehnfehrmoh

– sick_____
Tengo náuseas
tehngoh nahoosehahs

I've got a cold_____
Estoy acatarrado
ehstoy ahkahtahrrahdoh

It hurts here _____
Me duele aquí
meh dwehleh ahkee

I've been throwing up _____
He devuelto
eh dehbwehltoh

I've got... _____
Tengo molestias de...
tehngoh mohlehstyahs deh...

I'm running a _____ temperature of...degrees
Tengo...grados de fiebre
tehngoh...grahdohs deh fyehbreh

I've been stung by_____ a wasp
Me ha picado una avispa
meh ah peekahdoh oonah ahbeespah

I've been stung by an_____ insect
Me ha picado un insecto
meh ah peekahdoh oon eensehktoh

I've been bitten by _____ a dog
Me ha mordido un perro
meh ah mohrdeedoh oon pehrroh

I've been stung by_____ a jellyfish
Me ha picado una medusa
meh ah peekahdoh oonah mehdoosah

I've been bitten by _____ a snake	Me ha mordido una serpiente
	meh ah mohrdeedoh oonah sehrpyehnteh
I've been bitten by _____ an animal	Me ha picado un insecto
	meh ah peekahdoh oon eensehktoh
I've cut myself _____	Me he cortado
	meh eh kohrtahdoh
I've burned myself _____	Me he quemado
	meh eh kehmahdoh
I've grazed myself_____	Tengo una rozadura
	tehngoh oonah rohthahdoorah
I've had a fall _____	Me he caído
	meh eh kaheedoh
I've sprained my ankle_____	Me he torcido el tobillo
	meh eh tohrtheedoh ehl tohbeelyoh
I've come for the _____ morning-after pill	Vengo a que me dé una píldora del día después
	behngoh ah keh meh deh oonah peeldohrah dehl deeah dehspwehs

🖐️ .3 The consultation

¿Qué molestias tiene?_____	What seems to be the problem?
¿Cuánto hace que tiene estas _____ molestias?	How long have you had these symptoms?
¿Ha tenido estas molestias _____ anteriormente?	Have you had this trouble before?
¿Qué temperatura tiene? _____	How high is your temperature?
Desnúdese._____	Get undressed, please
Desvístase de la cintura para arriba _____	Strip to the waist, please
Allí puede quitarse la ropa_____	You can undress there
Descúbrase el brazo_____ izquierdo/derecho	Roll up your left/right sleeve, please
Recuéstese aquí _____	Lie down here, please
¿Le duele esto? _____	Does this hurt?
Respire hondo _____	Breathe deeply
Abra la boca_____	Open your mouth

Patient's medical history

I'm a diabetic _____	Soy diabético
	soy deeahbehteekoh
I have a heart condition____	Soy enfermo cardíaco
	soy ehnfehrmoh kahrdeeahkoh
I have asthma_____	Soy asmático
	soy ahsmahteekoh
I'm allergic to... _____	Soy alérgico a...
	soy ahlehrheekoh ah...
I'm...months pregnant _____	Estoy embarazada de...meses
	ehstoy ehmbahrahthadah deh...mehsehs
I'm on a diet _____	Sigo una dieta
	seegoh oonah dyehtah

Sickness

13

I'm on medication/ _____ the pill	Tomo medicamentos/la píldora *tohmoh mehdeekahmehntohs/lah peeldohrah*
I've had a heart attack _____ once before	He tenido un ataque cardíaco anteriormente *eh tehneedoh oon ahtahkeh kahrdeeahkoh ahntehryohrmehnteh*
I've had a(n)...operation ___	Me han operado del/de la... *meh ahn ohpehrahdoh dehl/deh lah...*
I've been ill recently _____	He estado enfermo hace poco *eh ehstahdoh ehnfehrmoh ahtheh pohkoh*
I've got an ulcer_____	Tengo una úlcera *tehngoh oonah oolthehrah*
I've got my period_____	Tengo la regla *tehngoh lah rehglah*

¿Padece alguna alergia?_____	Do you have any allergies?
¿Toma medicamentos?_____	Are you on any medication?
¿Sigue alguna dieta? _____	Are you on a diet?
¿Está embarazada? _____	Are you pregnant?
¿Está vacunado/a contra el tétanos?_____	Have you had a tetanus injection?

The diagnosis

No es nada grave _____	It's nothing serious
Se ha fracturado el/la..._____	Your...is broken
Se ha contusionado el/la..._____	You've got a/some bruised...
Se ha desgarrado el/la..._____	You've got (a) torn...
Tiene una inflamación_____	You've got an inflammation
Tiene apendicitis _____	You've got appendicitis
Tiene bronquitis _____	You've got bronchitis
Tiene una enfermedad venérea _____	You've got a venereal disease
Tiene gripe _____	You've got the flu
Ha tenido un ataque al corazón _____	You've had a heart attack
Tiene una infección virósica/_____ bacteriana	You've got an infection (viral..., bacterial...)
Tiene una pulmonía_____	You've got pneumonia
Tiene una úlcera _____	You've got an ulcer
Se ha distendido un músculo _____	You've pulled a muscle
Tiene una infección vaginal_____	You've got a vaginal infection
Tiene una intoxicación alimenticia _____	You've got food poisoning

Tiene una insolación _____	You've got sunstroke
Es alérgico a... _____	You're allergic to...
Está embarazada _____	You're pregnant
Quisiera hacerle un análisis de sangre/de orina/de materia fecal	I'd like to have your blood/urine/stools tested
Hay que suturar la herida_____	It needs stitching
Lo/la voy a derivar a un especialista/a ___ un hospital	I'm referring you to a specialist/sending you to hospital
Tiene que hacerse radiografías _____	You'll need to have some x-rays taken
Vuelva a tomar asiento en la sala de ____ espera	Could you wait in the waiting room, please?
Hay que operarlo/operarla_____	You'll need an operation

Is it contagious?_____	¿Es contagioso?
	ehs kohntah<u>h</u>yohsoh?
How long do I have to _____ stay...?	¿Hasta cuándo tengo que...?
	ahstah kwahndoh tehngoh keh...?
– in bed _____	¿Hasta cuándo tengo que guardar cama?
	ahstah kwahndoh tehngoh keh gwahrdahr kahmah?
– in hospital _____	¿Hasta cuándo tengo que quedarme en el hospital?
	ahstah kwahndoh tehngoh keh kehdahrmeh ehn ehl ohspeetahl?
Do I have to go on _____ a special diet?	¿Tengo que seguir alguna dieta?
	tehngoh keh sehgheer ahlgoonah dyehtah?
Am I allowed to travel? ____	¿Puedo viajar?
	pwehdoh byah<u>h</u>ahr?
Can I make a new _____ appointment?	¿Puedo volver a pedir hora?
	pwehdoh bohlbehr ah pehdeer ohrah?
When do I have to_____ come back?	¿Cuándo tengo que volver?
	kwahndoh tehngoh keh bohlbehr?
I'll come back _____ tomorrow	Vuelvo mañana
	bwehlboh mahnyahnah

Vuelva mañana/dentro de...días _____	Come back tomorrow/in...days' time

🔞 .4 Medication and prescriptions

How do I take this _____ medicine?	¿Cómo se toman estos medicamentos?
	kohmoh seh tohmahn ehstohs mehdeekahmehntohs?
How many capsules/ _____ drops/injections/ spoonfuls/tablets each time?	¿Cuántas cápsulas/gotas/inyecciones/ cucharadas/tabletas por vez?
	kwahntahs kahpsoolahs/gohtahs/eenyehkthyohnehs/koo chahrahdahs pohr behth?
How many times a day? ___	¿Cuántas veces al día?

I've forgotten my_____ medication. At home I take...	*kwahntahs behthehs ahl deeah?* Se me ha olvidado traer los medicamentos. En casa tomo... *seh meh ah olbeedahdoh trahehr lohs mehdeekahmehntohs. ehn kahsah tohmoh...*
Could you make out a _____ prescription for me?	¿Podría hacerme una receta? *pohdreeah ahthehrmeh oonah rehthehtah?*
Do you know a good _____	¿Me podría recomendar un buen dentista?

Voy a recetarle unos antibióticos/un_____ jarabe/un calmante/ unos analgésicos	I'm prescribing antibiotics/a mixture/a tranquillizer/pain killers
Tiene que guardar reposo _____	Have lots of rest
No tiene que salir a la calle _____	Stay indoors
Tiene que guardar cama_____	Stay in bed

---

antes de cada comida	inyecciones	tragar entero
before meals	injections	swallow whole
cápsulas	para uso externo	tabletas
capsules	exclusivamente	tablets
diluir en agua	not for internal use	tomar/ingerir
dissolve in water	ungüento	take
gotas	ointment	estos medicamentos
drops	aplicar/embadurnar	afectan la capacidad
cada...horas	rub on	de conducir
every...hours	cucharadas (soperas/	this medication
seguir la cura hasta	cucharaditas)	impairs your driving
el final	spoonfuls	...vez/veces cada 24
finish the course	(tablespoons/	horas
durante...días	tea-spoons)	...times a day
for...days		

13 .5 At the dentist's

dentist?	*meh pohdreeah rehkohmehndahr oon bwehn dehnteestah?*
Could you make a_____ dentist's appointment for me? It's urgent	¿Me podría pedir hora con el dentista? Es urgente *meh pohdreeah pehdeer ohrah kohn ehl dehnteestah? ehs oorhehnte*
Can I come in today,_____ please?	¿Me podría atender hoy mismo? *meh pohdreeah ahtehndehr oy meesmoh?*
I have (terrible)_____ toothache	Tengo (un terrible) dolor de muelas *tehngoh (oon tehrreebleh) dohlohr deh mwehlahs*
Could you prescribe/ _____ give me a painkiller?	¿Me podría recetar/dar un analgésico? *meh pohdreeah rehthehtahr/dahr oon ahnahlhehseekoh?*

A piece of my tooth _____	Se me ha caído un pedazo de un diente

105

has broken off	*seh meh ah kaheedoh oon pehdahthoh deh oon dyehnteh*
My filling's come out _____	Se me ha salido un empaste
	seh meh ah sahleedoh oon ehmpahsteh
I've got a broken crown___	Se me ha roto la corona
	seh meh ah rohtoh lah kohrohnah
I'd like/I don't want a _____ local anaesthetic	Quisiera que/no quiero que me ponga anestesia local
	keesyehrah keh/noh kyehroh keh meh pohngah ahnehstehsyah lohkahl
Can you do a makeshift___ repair job?	¿Me podría hacer un arreglo provisional?
	meh pohdreeah ahthehr oon ahrrehgloh prohbeesyohnahl?
I don't want this tooth _____ pulled	No quiero que me extraiga esta muela
	noh kyehroh keh meh ehxtraygah ehstah mwehlah
My dentures are broken. ___ Can you fix them?	Se me ha roto la dentadura postiza ¿Podría arreglármela?
	seh meh ah rohtoh lah dehntahdoorah pohsteethah. pohdreeah arrehglahrmehlah?

¿Qué diente/muela le duele?_____	Which tooth hurts?
Tiene un absceso _____	You've got an abscess
Tengo que tratarle el nervio _____	I'll have to do a root canal
Voy a ponerle anestesia local _____	I'm giving you a local anaesthetic
Tengo que empastarle/extraerle/ _____ pulirle este/esta...	I'll have to fill/pull this tooth/file this...down
Tengo que usar el torno _____	I'll have to drill
Abra la boca_____	Open wide, please
Cierre la boca_____	Close your mouth, please
Enjuáguese_____	Rinse, please
¿Le sigue doliendo?_____	Does it hurt still?

Sickness

13

In trouble

14 In trouble

14 .1 Asking for help

English	Spanish
Help! _____	¡Socorro!
	sohkohrroh!
Fire! _____	¡Fuego!
	fwehgoh!
Police! _____	¡Policía!
	pohleetheeah!
Quick! _____	¡Rápido!
	rahpeedoh!
Danger! _____	¡Peligro!
	pehleegroh!
Watch out! _____	¡Cuidado!
	kweedahdoh!
Stop! _____	¡Alto!
	ahltoh!
Be careful! _____	¡Cuidado!
	kweedahdoh!
Don't! _____	¡No, no!
	noh, noh!
Let go! _____	¡Suelte!
	swehlteh!
Stop that thief! _____	¡Al ladrón!
	ahl lahdrohn!
Could you help me, _____ please?	¿Podría ayudarme, por favor?
	pohdreeah ahyoodahrmeh, pohr fahbohr?
Where's the police _____ station/emergency exit/fire escape?	¿Dónde está la comisaría/la salida de emergencia/la escalera de incendios?
	dohndeh ehstah lah kohmeesahreeah/lah sahleedah deh ehmehrhehnthyah/lah ehskahlehrah deh eenthehndyohs?
Where's the nearest fire ___ extinguisher?	¿Dónde hay un extintor?
	dohndeh ay oon ehxteentohr?
Call the fire brigade! _____	¡Llamen a los bomberos!
	lyahmehn ah lohs bohmbehrohs!
Call the police! _____	¡Llamen a la policía!
	lyahmehn ah lah pohleetheeah!
Call an ambulance! _____	¡Llamen a una ambulancia!
	lyahmehn ah oonah ahmboolahnthyah!
Where's the nearest _____ phone?	¿Dónde hay un teléfono?
	dohndeh ay oon tehlehfohnoh?
Could I use your phone? ___	¿Podría llamar por teléfono?
	pohdreeah lyahmahr pohr tehlehfohnoh?
What's the emergency _____ number?	¿Cuál es el número de urgencias?
	kwahl ehs ehl noomehroh deh oorhehnthyahs?
What's the number for _____ the police?	¿Cuál es el número de la policía?
	kwahl ehs ehl noomehroh deh lah pohleetheeah?

In trouble

14

14.2 Loss

I've lost my purse/_____ wallet	Se me ha perdido el monedero/la cartera *seh meh ah pehrdeedoh ehl mohnehdehroh/lah kahrtehrah*
I left my...behind _____ yesterday	Ayer me dejé el/la... *ahyehr meh dehheh ehl/lah...*
I left my...here _____	Me he dejado el/la...aquí *meh eh dehhahdoh ehl/lah...ahkee*
Did you find my...? _____	¿Han encontrado mi...? *ahn ehnkohntrahdoh mee...?*
It was right here_____	Estaba aquí *ehstahbah ahkee*
It's quite valuable _____	Es muy valioso *ehs mwee bahlyohsoh*
Where's the lost_____ property office?	¿Dónde está la oficina de objetos perdidos? *dohndeh ehstah lah ohfeetheenah deh ohbhehtohs pehrdeedohs?*

14.3 Accidents

There's been an _____ accident	Ha habido un accidente *ah ahbeedoh oon ahktheedehnteh*
Someone's fallen into _____ the water	Se ha caído alguien al agua *seh ah kaheedoh ahlgyehn ahl ahgwah*
There's a fire_____	Hay un incendio *ay oon eenthehndyoh*
Is anyone hurt? _____	¿Hay algún herido? *ay ahlgoon ehreedoh?*
Some people have _____ been/no one's been injured	(No) hay heridos *(noh) ay ehreedohs*
There's someone in _____ the car/train still	Todavía queda alguien en el coche/tren *tohdahbeeah kehdah ahlgyehn ehn ehl kohcheh/trehn*
It's not too bad. Don't_____ worry	No es grave. No se preocupe *noh ehs grahbeh. noh seh prehohkoopeh*
Leave everything the _____ way it is, please	No toque nada *noh tohkeh nahdah*
I want to talk to the_____ police first	Primero quisiera hablar con la policía *preemehroh keesyehrah ahblahr kohn lah pohleetheeah*
I want to take a _____ photo first	Primero quisiera sacar una foto *preemehroh keesyehrah sahkahr oonah fohtoh*
Here's my name_____ and address	Aquí tiene mi nombre y dirección *ahkee tyehneh mee nohmbreh ee deerehkthyohn*
Could I have your _____ name and address?	¿Me da su nombre y dirección? *meh dah soo nohmbreh ee deerehkthyohn?*
Could I see some_____ identification/your insurance papers?	¿Me permite su carnet de identidad/sus papeles del seguro? *meh pehrmeeteh soo kahrneh deh eedehnteedahdh/soos pahpehlehs dehl sehgooroh?*

In trouble

14

Will you act as a _____ witness?	¿Le importaría hacer de testigo?
	leh eempohrtahreeah ahtehdeh tehsteegoh?
I need the details for _____ the insurance	Necesito los datos para el seguro
	nehthehseetoh lohs dahtohs pahrah ehl sehgooroh
Are you insured? _____	¿Está asegurado?
	ehstah ahsehgoorahdoh?
Third party or _____ comprehensive?	¿Responsabilidad civil o contra todo riesgo?
	rehspohnsahbeeleedahdh theebeel oh kohntrah tohdoh ryehsgoh?
Could you sign here, _____ please?	Firme aquí, por favor
	feermeh ahkee, pohr fahbohr

🕘 .4 Theft

I've been robbed _____	Me han robado
	meh ahn rohbahdoh
My...has been stolen _____	Me han robado el/la...
	meh ahn rohbahdoh ehl/lah...
My car's been _____ broken into	Me han abierto el coche
	meh ahn ahbyehrtoh ehl kohcheh

🕘 .5 Missing person

I've lost my child/ _____ grandmother	Se ha perdido mi hijo/mi hija/mi abuela
	seh ah pehrdeedoh mee eehoh/mee eehah/mee ahbwehlah
Could you help me _____ find him/her?	¿Podría ayudarme a buscarlo/la?
	pohdreeah ahyoodahrmeh ah booskahrloh/lah?
Have you seen a _____ small child?	¿Ha visto a un niño pequeño/a una niña pequeña?
	ah veestoh ah oon neenyoh pehkehnyoh/ah oonah neenyah pehkehnyah?
He's/she's...years old _____	Tiene...años
	tyehneh...ahnyohs
He's/she's got _____ short/long/blond/red/ brown/black/ grey/curly/ straight/frizzy hair	Tiene el pelo corto/largo/rubio/rojo/castaño/negro/ canoso/rizado/liso/crespo
	tyehneh ehl pehloh kohrtoh/lahrgoh/roobyoh/kahstahnyoh/neh groh/kahnohsoh/reethahdoh/leesoh/krehspoh
with a ponytail _____	con cola de caballo
	kohn kohlah deh kahbahlyoh
with plaits _____	con trenzas
	kohn trehnthahs
in a bun _____	con moño
	kohn mohnyoh
He's/she's got _____ blue/brown/green eyes	Tiene ojos azules/marrones/verdes
	tyehneh ohhohs ahthoolehs/mahrrohnehs/behrdehs

He's wearing swimming ___ | Lleva bañador/botas de montaña
trunks/mountaineering | *lyehbah bahnyahdohr/bohtahs deh*
boots | *mohntahnyah*
with/without glasses/ _____ | con/sin gafas/bolso
a bag | *kohn/seen gahfahs/bohlsoh*
tall/short_____ | alto/bajito
 | *ahltoh/bahheetoh*

This is a photo of _____ | Esta es su foto
him/her | *ehstah ehs soo fohtoh*
He/she must be lost _____ | Seguramente se habrá perdido
 | *sehgoorahmehnteh seh ahbrah pehrdeedoh*

14 .6 The police

An arrest

Los papeles del coche, por favor _____	Your registration papers, please
Conducía demasiado rápido _____	You were speeding
Tiene mal aparcado el coche_____	You're not allowed to park here
No ha puesto monedas en el _____ parquímetro	You haven't put money in the meter
No le funcionan los faros_____	Your lights aren't working
Le vamos a poner una multa de..._____ pesetas	That's a...pesetas fine
¿Va a pagar la multa en el acto? _____	Do you want to pay on the spot?
Tiene que pagar en el acto_____	You'll have to pay on the spot

I don't speak Spanish_____ | No hablo español
 | *noh ahbloh ehspahnyohl*
I didn't see the sign _____ | No he visto el cartel
 | *noh eh beestoh ehl kahrtehl*
I don't understand_____ | No entiendo lo que dice
what it says | *noh ehntyehndoh loh keh deetheh*
I was only doing..._____ | Sólo iba a...kilómetros por hora
kilometres an hour | *sohloh eebah ah...keelohmehtrohs pohr*
 | *ohrah*
I'll have my car checked ___ | Haré revisar el coche
 | *ahreh rehbeesahr ehl kohcheh*
I was blinded by _____ | Me cegó un coche que venía de frente
oncoming lights | *meh thehgoh oon kohcheh keh behneeah*
 | *deh frehnteh*

At the police station

I want to report a_____ | Vengo a hacer la denuncia de un
collision/missing | choque/un extravío/una violación
person/rape | *behngoh ah ahtehr lah dehnoonthyah deh*
 | *oon chohkeh/oon ehxtrahbeeoh/oonah*
 | *beeohlahthyohn*

Could you make out _____ ¿Podría hacer un atestado?
a report, please? *pohdreeah ahtehr oon ahtehstahdoh?*
Could I have a copy _____ ¿Me podría dar una copia para el seguro?
for the insurance? *meh pohdreeah dahr oonah kohpyah pahrah ehl sehgooroh?*
I've lost everything _____ He perdido todo
eh pehrdeedoh tohdoh

¿Dónde ha sido? _____ Where did it happen?
¿Qué se le ha perdido? _____ What's missing?
¿Qué le han robado? _____ What's been taken?
¿Me permite su documento de_____ Could I see some
identidad? identification?
¿A qué hora ocurrió?_____ What time did it happen?
¿Quiénes estuvieron implicados? _____ Who was involved?
¿Hay testigos? _____ Are there any witnesses?
Rellene este formulario_____ Fill this out, please
Firme aquí, por favor_____ Sign here, please
¿Quiere un intérprete? _____ Do you want an
interpreter?

I'd like an interpreter _____ Quisiera un intérprete
keesyehrah oon eentehrprehteh
I'm innocent _____ Soy inocente
soy eenohthehnteh
I don't know anything _____ No sé nada
about it *noh seh nahdah*
I want to speak to _____ Quisiera hablar con alguien de...
someone... *keesyehrah ahblahr kohn ahlgyehn deh...*
from the British _____ Quisiera hablar con alguien del Consulado
consulate Británico
keesyehrah ahblahr kohn ahlgyehn dehl kohnsoolahdoh breetahneekoh
I need to see someone _____ Quisiera hablar con alguien de la
from the British Embajada Británica
embassy *keesyehrah ahblahr kohn ahlgyehn deh lah ehmbah__h__ahdah breetahneekah*
I want a lawyer who_____ Quisiera un abogado que hable inglés
speaks English *keesyehrah oon ahbohgahdoh keh ahbleh eenglehs*

In trouble

14

15

Word list

Word list English - Spanish

● **This word list** is meant to supplement the previous chapters.
Nouns are always accompanied by the Spanish definite article in order
to indicate whether it is a masculine (el) or feminine (la) word.
In a number of cases, words not contained in this list can be found
elsewhere in this booklet, namely alongside the diagrams of the car,
the bicycle and the tent. Many food terms can be found in the Spanish-
English list in 4.7.

A

a little	un poco	*oon pohkoh*
above (up)	arriba	*ahrreebah*
abroad	el extranjero	*ehl ehxtrahnhehroh*
accident	el accidente	*ehl ahktheedehnteh*
adder	la víbora	*la veebohrah*
addition	la suma	*lah soomah*
address	la dirección	*lah deerehkthyohn*
admission	la entrada	*lah ehntrahdah*
admission price	el precio de entrada	*ehl prehthyoh deh lah ehntrahdah*
admission ticket	la entrada	*lah ehntrahdah*
advice	el consejo	*ehl kohnsehhoh*
after	después de	*dehspwehs deh*
afternoon (in the)	(por) la tarde	*(pohr) lah tahrdeh*
aftershave	la loción para después del afeitado	*lah lohthyohn pahrah dehspwehs dehl ahfehytahdoh*
again	de nuevo	*deh nwehboh*
against	contra	*kohntrah*
age	la edad	*lah ehdahdh*
Aids	el Sida	*ehl seedah*
air conditioning	el aire acondicionado	*ehl ayreh ahkohndeethyohnahdoh*
air mattress	el colchón neumático	*ehl kohlchohn nehoomahteekoh*
air sickness bag	bolsita para el mareo	*bohlseetah pahrah ehl mahrehoh*
aircraft	el avión	*ehl ahbyohn*
airport	el aeropuerto	*ehl ahehrohpwehrtoh*
alarm	la alarma	*lah ahlahrmah*
alarm clock	el despertador	*ehl dehspehrtahdohr*
alcohol	el alcohol	*ehl ahlkohohl*
all the time	cada vez	*kahdah behth*
allergic	alérgico	*ahlehrheekoh*
alone	solo	*sohloh*
always	siempre	*syehmpreh*
ambulance	la ambulancia	*lah ahmboolahnthyah*
amount	el importe	*ehl eempohrteh*
amusement park	el parque de atracciones	*ehl pahrkeh deh ahtrahkthyohnehs*
anaesthetize	anestesiar	*ahnehstehsyahr*
anchovy	la anchoa	*lah ahnchohah*
angry	enfadado	*ehnfahdahdoh*
animal	el animal	*ehl ahneemahl*
ankle	el tobillo	*ehl tohbeelyoh*
answer	la respuesta	*lah rehspwehstah*

ant	la hormiga	*lah ohrmeegah*
antibiotics	los antibióticos	*lohs ahnteebyohteekohs*
antifreeze	el anticongelante	*ehl ahnteekohn<u>h</u>ehlahnteh*
antique	antiguo	*ahnteegwoh*
antiques	las antigüedades	*lahs ahnteegwehdahdehs*
anus	el ano	*ehl ahnoh*
apartment	el apartamento	*ehl ahpahrtahmehntoh*
aperitif	el aperitivo	*ehl ahpehreeteeboh*
apologies	las disculpas	*lahs deeskoolpahs*
apple	la manzana	*lah mahnthahnah*
apple juice	el zumo de manzana	*ehl thoomoh deh mahnthahnah*
apple pie	la tarta de manzana	*lah tahrtah deh mahnthahnah*
apple sauce	el puré de manzanas	*ehl pooreh deh mahnthahnahs*
appointment	la hora	*lah ohrah*
approximately	más o menos	*mahs oh mehnohs*
April	abril	*ahbreel*
archbishop	el arzobispo	*ehl ahrthohbeespoh*
architecture	la arquitectura	*lah ahrkeetehktoorah*
area	los alrededores	*lohs ahlrehdehdohrehs*
arm	el brazo	*ehl brahthoh*
arrange to meet	quedar	*kehdahr*
arrive	llegar	*lyehgahr*
arrow	la flecha	*lah flehchah*
art	el arte	*ehl ahrteh*
artery	la arteria	*lah ahrtehryah*
artichokes	las alcachofas	*lahs ahlkahchohfahs*
article	el artículo	*ehl ahrteekooloh*
artificial respiration	la respiración artificial	*lah rehspeerahthyohn ahrteefeethyahl*
arts and crafts	la artesanía	*lah ahrtehsahneeah*
ashtray	el cenicero	*ehl thehneethehroh*
ask (a question)	preguntar	*prehgoontahr*
ask for	pedir	*pehdeer*
asparagus	los espárragos	*lohs ehspahrrahgohs*
aspirin	la aspirina	*lah ahspeereenah*
assault	la agresión	*lah ahgrehsyohn*
aubergine	la berenjena	*lah behrehn<u>h</u>ehnah*
August	agosto	*ahgohstoh*
automatic	automático	*ahootohmahteekoh*
automatic car	el coche con cambio automático	*ehl kohcheh kohn kahmbyoh ahootohmahteekoh*
autumn	el otoño	*ehl ohtohnyoh*
avalanche	el alud	*ehl ahloodh*
awake (adj.)	despierto	*dehspyehrtoh*
awning	el toldo	*ehl tohldoh*

15

B

baby	el bebé	*ehl behbeh*
baby food	la comida para bebés	*lah kohmeedah pahrah behbehs*
babysitter	la niñera	*lah neenyehrah*
back (at the)	atrás	*ahtrahs*
back	la espalda	*lah ehspahldah*
backpack	la mochila	*lah mohcheelah*
bacon	el tocino	*ehl tohtheenoh*
bad	mal, malo	*mahl, mahloh*
bag	la bolsa	*lah bohlsah*
baker	la panadería	*lah pahnahdehreeah*
balcony (theatre)	el palco (alto)	*ehl pahlkoh (ahltoh)*
balcony (to building)	el balcón	*ehl bahlkohn*
ball	la pelota	*lah pehlohtah*
ballet	el ballet	*ehl bahleh*
ballpoint pen	el bolígrafo	*ehl bohleegrahfoh*
banana	el plátano	*ehl plahtahnoh*
bandage	la gasa	*lah gahsah*
bank (river)	la orilla	*lah ohreelyah*
bank	el banco	*ehl bahnkoh*
bank card	la tarjeta del banco	*lah tahr<u>h</u>ehtah dehl bahnkoh*
bar (café)	el bar	*ehl bahr*
bar (drinks' cabinet)	la barra	*lah bahrrah*
bar	la barra	*lah bahrrah*
barbecue	la barbacoa	*lah bahrbahkohah*
basketball	el baloncesto	*ehl bahlohnthehstoh*
bath	el baño	*ehl bahnyoh*
bath attendant	el bañista	*ehl bahnyeestah*
bath foam	el gel de baño	*ehl <u>h</u>ehl deh bahnyoh*
bath towel	la toalla de baño	*lah tohahlyah deh bahnyoh*
bathing cap	el gorro de baño	*ehl gohrroh deh bahnyoh*
bathing cubicle	la caseta	*lah kahsehtah*
bathing suit	el bañador	*ehl bahnyahdohr*
bathroom	el cuarto de baño	*ehl kwahrtoh deh bahnyoh*
battery (car)	la batería	*lah bahtehreeah*
battery	la pila	*lah peelah*
beach	la playa	*lah plahyah*
beans	las judías blancas	*lahs <u>h</u>oodeeahs blahnkahs*
beautiful	bonito	*bohneetoh*
beauty parlour	el salón de belleza	*ehl sahlohn deh behlyehthah*
bed	la cama	*lah kahmah*
bee	la abeja	*lah ahbeh<u>h</u>ah*
beef	la carne de vaca	*lah kahrneh deh bahkah*
beer	la cerveza	*lah thehrbehthah*
beetroot	la remolacha	*lah rehmohlahchah*
begin	empezar	*ehmpehthahr*
beginner	el principiante	*ehl preentheepyahnteh*
behind	atrás	*ahtrahs*
Belgian (f)	la belga	*lah behlgah*
Belgian (m)	el belga	*ehl behlgah*

15 **Word list**

Belgium	Bélgica	*behlheekah*
bellboy	el mozo de cuerda	*ehl mohthoh deh kwehrdah*
belt	el cinturón	*ehl theentoorohn*
berth	la litera	*lah leetehrah*
better	mejor	*mehhohr*
bicarb	el bicarbonato	*ehl beekahrbohnahtoh*
bicycle	la bicicleta	*lah beetheeklehtah*
bicycle pump	el inflador	*ehl eenflahdohr*
bicycle repairman	el mecánico de bicicletas	*ehl mehkahneekoh deh beetheeklehtahs*
bikini	el bikini	*ehl beekeenee*
bill	la cuenta	*lah kwehntah*
billiards, to play	el juego de billar	*ehl hwehgoh deh beelyahr*
birthday (to have a)	cumplir años	*koompleer ahnyohs*
birthday	el cumpleaños	*ehl koomplehahnyohs*
biscuit	la galleta	*lah gahlyehtah*
bite	morder	*mohrdehr*
bitter	amargo	*ahmahrgoh*
black	negro	*nehgroh*
bland	soso	*sohsoh*
blanket	la manta	*lah mahntah*
bleach	teñir de rubio	*tehnyeer deh roobyoh*
blister	la ampolla	*lah ahmpohlyah*
blond	rubio	*roobyoh*
blood	la sangre	*lah sahngreh*
blood pressure	la tensión sanguínea	*lah tehnsyohn sahngheenehah*
blouse	la blusa	*lah bloosah*
blow dry	secar a mano	*sehkahr ah mahnoh*
blue	azul	*ahthool*
boat	el barco	*ehl bahrkoh*
body	el cuerpo	*ehl kwehrpoh*
body milk	la leche corporal	*lah lehcheh kohrpohrahl*
boiled	cocido	*kohtheedoh*
boiled ham	el jamón de York	*ehl hahmohn deh yohrk*
bonbon	el bombón	*ehl bohmbohn*
bone	el hueso	*ehl wehsoh*
bonnet	el capó	*ehl kahpoh*
book (verb)	reservar	*rehsehrbahr*
book	el libro	*ehl leebroh*
booked	reservado	*rehsehrbahdoh*
booking office	la taquilla	*lah tahkeelyah*
bookshop	la librería	*lah leebrehreeah*
border	la frontera	*lah frohntehrah*
bored (be)	aburrirse	*ahboorreerseh*
boring	aburrido	*ahboorreedoh*
born	nacido	*nahtheedoh*
botanical gardens	el jardín botánico	*ehl hahrdeen bohtahneekoh*
both	ambos/ambas	*ahmbohs/ahmbahs*
bottle (baby's)	el biberón	*ehl beebehrohn*
bottle	la botella	*lah bohtehlyah*
bottle-warmer	el calentador de biberones	*ehl kahlehntahdohr de beebehrohnehs*
box (in theatre)	el palco	*ehl pahlkoh*

box	la caja	*kahhah*
boy	el chico	*ehl cheekoh*
bra	el sujetador	*ehl soohehtahdohr*
bracelet	la pulsera	*lah poolsehrah*
braised	estofado	*ehstohfahdoh*
brake	el freno	*ehl frehnoh*
brake fluid	el líquido de frenos	*ehl leekeedoh deh frehnohs*
bread	el pan	*ehl pahn*
bread roll	el panecillo	*ehl pahnehtheelyoh*
breakdown recovery	el auxilio en carretera	*ehl ahooxeelyoh ehn kahrrehtehrah*
break (limb)	fracturarse	*frahktoorahrseh*
breakfast	el desayuno	*ehl dehsahyoonoh*
breast	el pecho	*ehl pehchoh*
bridge	el puente	*ehl pwehnteh*
bring	llevar	*lyehbahr*
brochure	el folleto	*ehl fohlyehtoh*
broken	roto, estropeado	*rohtoh, ehstrohpehahdoh*
broth	el caldo	*ehl kahldoh*
brother	el hermano	*ehl ehrmahnoh*
brown	marrón	*mahrrohn*
bruise (verb)	contusionarse	*kohntoosyohnahrseh*
brush	el cepillo	*ehl thehpeelyoh*
Brussels sprouts	las coles de Bruselas	*lahs kohlehs deh broosehlahs*
bucket	el cubo	*ehl kooboh*
bug	el bicho	*ehl beechoh*
building	el edificio	*ehl ehdeefeethyoh*
bullfight	la corrida de toros	*lah kohrreedah deh tohrohs*
buoy	la boya	*lah boyah*
burglary	el robo en una casa	*ehl rohboh ehn oonah kahsah*
burn (verb)	quemar	*kehmahr*
burn	la quemadura	*lah kehmahdoorah*
burnt	quemado	*kehmahdoh*
bus	el autobús	*ehl ahootohboos*
bus station	la estación de autobuses	*lah ehstahthyohn deh ahootohboos*
bus stop	la parada de autobús	*lah pahrahdah deh ahootohboos*
business class	la clase preferente	*lah klahseh prehfehrehnteh*
business trip	el viaje de negocios	*ehl byahheh deh nehgohthyohs*
busy (crowded)	hay mucha gente	*ay moochah hehnteh*
butane camping gas	el gas butano	*ehl gahs bootahnoh*
butcher's	la carnicería	*lah kahrneethehreeah*
butter	la mantequilla	*lah mahntehkeelyah*
button	el botón	*ehl bohtohn*
buy	comprar	*kohmprahr*
by airmail	el correo aéreo/ vía aérea	*ehl kohrrehoh ahehrehoh/beeah ahehrehah*

c

cabbage	la col, la berza	*lah kohl, lah behrthah*
cabin	la cabaña	*lah kahbahnyah*
cake	el pastel	*ehl pahstehl*
cake shop	la pastelería, la confitería	*lah pahstehlehreeah, lah kohnfeetehreeah*
call (by phone)	llamar por teléfono	*lyahmahr pohr tehlehfohnoh*
called, to be	llamarse	*lyahmahrseh*
camera	la máquina fotográfica	*lah mahkeenah fohtohgrahfeekah*
camp	acampar	*ahkahmpahr*
camp shop	la tienda del camping	*lah tyehndah dehl kahmpeen*
camp site	el camping	*ehl kahmpeen*
camper van	el autocaravana	*ehl ahootohkahrah-bahnah*
campfire	la fogata	*lah fohgahtah*
camping guide	la guía de camping	*lah gheeah deh kahmpeen*
camping permit	el permiso de acampar	*ehl pehrmeesoh deh ahkahmpahr*
canal boat	el barco de excursión	*ehl bahrkoh deh ehxkoorsyohn*
cancel	cancelar	*kahnthehlahr*
candle	la vela	*lah behlah*
canoe	la piragua	*lah peerahgwah*
canoeing	el piragüismo	*ehl peerahgweesmoh*
cap (hat)	el gorro	*ehl gohrroh*
car	el coche	*ehl kohcheh*
car deck	la bodega para coches	*lah bohdehgah pahrah kohchehs*
car documents	los papeles del coche	*lohs pahpehlehs dehl kohcheh*
car registration	el permiso de circulación	*ehl pehrmeesoh deh theerkoolahthyohn*
car trouble	la avería	*lah ahbehreeah*
carafe	la jarra	*lah <u>h</u>ahrrah*
caravan	la caravana	*lah kahrahbahnah*
cardigan	el chaleco	*ehl chahlehkoh*
careful	con cuidado	*kohn kweedahdoh*
carrot	la zanahoria	*lah thahnahohryah*
carton	el cartón	*ehl kahrtohn*
cartridge	el carrete de cassette	*ehl kahrrehteh deh kahseht*
cascade	la cascada	*lah kahskahdah*
cash desk	la caja	*lah kah<u>h</u>ah*
casino	el casino	*ehl kahseenoh*
cassette	la cassette	*lah kahseht*
castle	el castillo	*ehl kahsteelyoh*
cat	el gato	*ehl gahtoh*
catalogue	el catálogo	*ehl kahtahlohgoh*
cathedral	la catedral	*lah kahtehdrahl*
cauliflower	la coliflor	*lah kohleeflohr*
cave	la gruta	*lah grootah*
CD	el compact disc	*ehl kohmpahkt deesk*

Word list

15

celebrate	celebrar una fiesta	*thehlehbrahr oonah fyehsta*
cellotape	la celo	*lah thehloh*
cemetery	el cementerio	*ehl thehmehntehryoh*
centimetre	centímetro(s)	*thehnteemehtroh(s)*
central heating	la calefacción central	*lah kahlehfakthyohn thehntrahl*
centre (in the)	en el centro/ medio	*ehn ehl thehntroh/ mehdyoh*
centre	el centro	*ehl thehntroh*
chair	la silla	*lah seelyah*
chambermaid	la camarera	*lah kahmahrehrah*
chamois	la gamuza	*lah gahmoothah*
champagne	el champán/el cava	*ehl chahmpahn/ehl kahbah*
change (from paying)	la vuelta	*lah bwehltah*
change (train/plane etc.)	hacer trasbordo	*ahthehr trahsbohrdoh*
change (verb)	cambiar	*kahmbyahr*
change the baby's nappy	cambiar los pañales	*kahmbyahr lohs pahnyahlehs*
change the oil	cambiar el aceite	*kahmbyahr ehl ahtheyteh*
chapel	la capilla	*lah kahpeelyah*
charter flight	el vuelo chárter	*ehl bwehloh chahrtehr*
chat up	ligar	*leegahr*
check (verb)	controlar	*kohntrohlahr*
check in	facturar	*frahktoorahr*
cheers	salud	*sahloodh*
cheese (tasty, mild)	el queso (añejo, blando)	*ehl kehsoh (ahnyeh<u>h</u>oh, blahndoh)*
chef	el jefe	*ehl <u>h</u>ehfeh*
chemist	la droguería	*lah drohguehreeah*
cheque	el cheque	*ehl chehkeh*
cherries	las cerezas	*lahs thehrehthahs*
chess (play)	jugar al ajedrez	*<u>h</u>oogahr ahl a<u>h</u>ehdreth*
chewing gum	el chicle	*ehl cheekleh*
chicken	el pollo	*ehl pohlyoh*
chicory	las endivias	*lahs ehndeebyahs*
child	el hijo, el niño	*ehl ee<u>h</u>oh, ehl neenyoh*
child seat	el asiento para niños	*ehl ahsyehntoh pahrah neenyohs*
child's seat	el sillín para niños	*ehl seelyeen pahrah neenyohs*
chilled	refrigerado	*rehfree<u>h</u>ehrahdoh*
chin	la barbilla	*lah bahrbeelyah*
chips/crisps	las patatas fritas	*lahs pahtahtahs freetahs*
chocolate	el chocolate	*ehl chohkohlahteh*
choose	elegir/escoger	*ehleh<u>h</u>eer/ehskoh<u>h</u>ehr*
chop	la chuleta	*la choolehtah*
christian name	el nombre	*ehl nohmbreh*
church	la iglesia	*lah eeglehsyah*
church service	el servicio religioso	*ehl sehrbeethyoh rehlee<u>h</u>yohsoh*
cigar	el puro	*ehl pooroh*
cigar shop	el estanco	*ehl ehstahnkoh*
cigarette	el cigarrillo	*ehl theegahrreelyoh*

15 Word list

cigarette paper	el papel de fumar	*ehl pahpehl deh foomahr*
cine camera	la filmadora	*lah feelmahdohrah*
circle	el círculo	*ehl theerkooloh*
circus	el circo	*ehl theerkoh*
city map	el plano	*ehl plahnoh*
classic/classical	clásica	*klahseekah*
clean (adj.)	limpio	*leempyoh*
clean (verb)	limpiar	*leempyahr*
clear (adj.)	claro	*klahroh*
clearance	la liquidación	*lah leekeedahthyohn*
closed	cerrado	*thehrrahdoh*
closed off	(la carretera) cerrada	*(lah kahrrehtehrah) thehrrahdah*
clothes	la ropa	*lah rohpah*
clothes hanger	la percha	*lah pehrchah*
clothes peg	la pinza para la ropa	*lah peenthah pahrah lah rohpah*
coat	el abrigo	*ehl ahbreegoh*
cockroach	la cucaracha	*lah kookahrahchah*
cod	el bacalao (fresco)	*ehl bahkahlahoh (frehskoh)*
coffee	el café	*ehl kahfeh*
coffee creamer	la crema para el café	*lah krehmah pahrah ehl kahfeh*
coffee filter	el filtro de café	*ehl feeltroh deh kahfeh*
cognac	el coñac	*ehl kohnyah*
cold	frío	*freeoh*
cold	el constipado	*ehl kohnsteepahdoh*
cold cuts	los fiambres	*lohs fyahmbrehs*
collarbone	la clavícula	*lah klahbeekoolah*
colleague	el/la colega	*ehl/lah kohlehgah*
collision	el choque	*ehl chohkeh*
cologne	el agua de tocador	*ehl ahgwah deh tohkahdohr*
colour	el color	*ehl kohlohr*
colour TV	el televisor color	*ehl tehlehbeesohr kohlohr*
coloured pencils	los lápices de colores	*lohs lahpeethehs deh kohlohrehs*
colouring book	el libro para colorear	*ehl leebroh pahrah kohlohrehahr*
comb	el peine	*ehl peheeneh*
come	venir	*behneer*
compartment	el compartimiento	*ehl kohmpahrteemyehntoh*
complaint (medical)	la molestia	*lah mohlehstyah*
complaint	la queja	*lah keh<u>h</u>ah*
complaints book	el libro de reclamaciones	*ehl leebroh deh rehklahmahthyohnehs*
completely	del todo	*dehl tohdoh*
compliment	el cumplido	*ehl koompleedoh*
compulsory	obligatorio	*ohbleegahtohryoh*
concert	el concierto	*ehl kohnthyehrtoh*
concert hall	la sala de conciertos	*lah sahlah deh kohnthyehrtohs*

concussion	la conmoción cerebral	lah kohnmohthyohn thehrehbrahl
condiments	los condimentos	lohs kohndeemehntohs
condom	el condón	ehl kohndohn
congratulate	felicitar	fehleetheetahr
connection	el enlace	ehl ehnlahtheh
constipation	el estreñimiento	ehl ehstrehnyeemyehntoh
consulate	el consulado	ehl kohnsoolahdoh
consultation	la consulta	lah kohnsooltah
contact lens	la lentilla	lah lehnteelyah
contact lens solution	el líquido para las lentillas	ehl leekeedoh pahrah lahs lehnteelyahs
contagious	contagioso	kohntah<u>h</u>yohsoh
contest	el concurso	ehl kohnkoorsoh
contraceptive	el anticonceptivo	ehl ahnteekohn-thehpteeboh
contraceptive pill	la píldora anticonceptiva	ah peeldohrah lahnteekohnthehpteebah
convent	el convento	ehl kohnbehntoh
cook (verb)	cocinar	kohtheenahr
cook	el cocinero	ehl kohtheenehroh
copper	el cobre	ehl kohbreh
copy	la copia	lah kohpyah
corkscrew	el sacacorchos	ehl sahkahkohrchohs
corn flour	la maicena	lah maythehnah
corner	el rincón	ehl reenkohn
correct	correcto	kohrrehktoh
correspond	cartearse	kahrtehahrseh
corridor	el pasillo	ehl pahseelyoh
costume	el traje	ehl trah<u>h</u>eh
cot	la cuna	lah koonah
cotton	el algodón	ehl ahlgohdohn
cotton wool	el algodón	ehl ahlgohdohn
cough	la tos	lah tohs
cough mixture	el jarabe para la tos	ehl <u>h</u>ahrahbeh pahrah lah tohs
counter	el mostrador	ehl mohstrahdohr
country	el país	ehl pahees
country code	el indicativo del país	ehl eendeekahteeboh dehl pahees
country(side)	el campo	ehl kahmpoh
courgette	el calabacín	ehl kahlahbahtheen
course (of treatment)	la cura	lah koorah
cousin (f)	la prima	lah preemah
cousin (m)	el primo	ehl preemoh
crab	el cangrejo	ehl kahngre<u>h</u>oh
cream	la crema, la nata	lah krehmah, lah nahtah
credit card	la tarjeta de crédito	lah tahr<u>h</u>ehtah deh krehdeetoh
crisps/chips	las patatas fritas	lahs pahtahtahs freetahs
croissant	el croissant	ehl krwahsahn
cross the road	cruzar la calle	kroothahr lah kahlyeh
cross-country run	la pista de esquí de fondo	lah peestah deh ehskee deh fohndoh

cross-country skiing	el esquí de fondo	*ehl ehskee deh fohndoh*
cross-country skis	los esquís de fondo	*lohs ehskees deh fohndoh*
crossing (journey)	la travesía	*lah trahbehseeah*
cry (verb)	llorar	*lyohrahr*
cubic metre(s)	metro(s) cúbico(s)	*mehtroh(s) koobeekoh(s)*
cucumber	el pepino	*ehl pehpeenoh*
cuddly toy	el animal de peluche	*ehl ahneemahl deh pehloocheh*
cuff links	los gemelos	*lohs hehmehlohs*
culottes	la falda-pantalón	*lah fahldah pahntahlohn*
cup	la taza	*lah tahthah*
curly	rizado	*reethahdoh*
current	la corriente	*lah kohrryehnteh*
cushion	el cojín	*ehl cohheen*
custard	las natillas	*lahs nahteelyahs*
customary	habitual	*ahbeetwahl*
customs	la aduana	*lah ahdwahna*
customs check	el control de aduanas	*ehl kohntrohl deh ahdwahnahs*
cut (verb)	cortar	*kohrtahr*
cutlery	los cubiertos	*lohs koobyehrtohs*
cycling	montar en bicicleta	*mohntahr ehn beetheeklehtah*

D

dairy products	los productos lácteos	*lohs prodooktohs lahktehohs*
damaged	dañado, estropeado	*dahnyahdoh, ehstrohpehahdoh*
dance	bailar	*bahylahr*
dandruff	la caspa	*lah kahspah*
danger	el peligro	*ehl pehleegroh*
dangerous	peligroso	*pehleegrohsoh*
dark	oscuro	*ohskooroh*
date	la cita	*lah theetah*
daughter	la hija	*lah eehah*
day	el día, las 24 horas	*ehl deeah, lahs beheenteekwahtroh ohrahs*
day before yesterday	anteayer	*ahntehahyehr*
dead	muerto	*mwehrtoh*
decaffeinated	sin cafeína	*seen kahfeheenah*
December	diciembre	*deethyehmbreh*
deck chair	el sillón de playa	*ehl seelyohn deh plahyah*
declare(customs)	declarar	*dehklahrahr*
deep	hondo	*ohndoh*
deep sea diving	el buceo	*ehl boothehoh*
degrees	los grados	*lohs grahdohs*
delay	el retraso	*ehl rehtrahsoh*
delicious	delicioso	*dehleethyohsoh*
dentist	el dentista	*ehl dehnteestah*
dentures	la dentadura postiza	*lah dehntahdoorah pohsteethah*

deodorant	el desodorante	*ehl dehsohdohrahnteh*
department	la sección	*lah sehkthyohn*
department stores	los grandes almacenes	*lohs grahndehs ahlmahthehnehs*
departure	la partida	*lah pahrteedah*
departure time	la hora de salida	*lah ohrah deh sahleedah*
depilatory cream	la crema depilatoria	*lah krehmah dehpeelahtohryah*
deposit (in)	en consigna	*ehn kohnseegnah*
deposit	la fianza	*lah fyahnzah*
dessert	el postre	*ehl pohstreh*
destination	el destino, el punto final	*ehl dehsteenoh, ehl poontoh feenahl*
develop (photos)	revelar	*rehbehlahr*
diabetic	el diabético	*ehl dyahbehteekoh*
dial (verb)	marcar	*mahrkahr*
diamond	el diamante	*ehl deeahmahnteh*
diarrhoea	la diarrea	*lah deeahrrehah*
dictionary	el diccionario	*ehl deekthyohnahryoh*
diesel	el gasóleo	*ehl gahsohlehoh*
diet	la dieta	*lah dyehtah*
difficulty	la dificultad	*lah deefeekooltahdh*
dining room	el comedor	*ehl kohmehdohr*
dining/buffet car	el coche restaurante	*ehl kohcheh rehstahoorahnteh*
dinner (to have)	cenar	*thehnahr*
dinner	la cena, la comida	*lah thehnah, lah kohmeedah*
dinner jacket	el smoking	*ehl smohkeen*
direction	la dirección	*lah deerehkthyohn*
directly	directo	*deerehktoh*
dirty	sucio	*soothyoh*
disabled person	el minusválido	*ehl meenoosbahleedoh*
disappearance	la desaparición	*lah dehsahpahreethyohn*
disco	la discoteca	*lah deeskohtehkah*
discount	el descuento	*ehl dehskwehntoh*
dish	el plato	*ehl plahtoh*
dish of the day	el plato del día	*ehl plahtoh dehl deeah*
disinfectant	el desinfectante	*ehl dehseenfehktahnteh*
distance	la distancia	*lah deestahnthyah*
distilled water	el agua destilada	*ehl ahgwah dehsteelahdah*
disturb	molestar	*mohlehstahr*
disturbance	el fallo	*ehl fahlyoh*
dive (verb)	bucear	*boothehahr*
diving	el buceo	*ehl boothehoh*
diving board	el trampolín	*ehl trahmpohleen*
diving gear	el equipo de buzo	*ehl ehkeepoh deh boothoh*
divorced	divorciado	*deebohrthyahdoh*
DIY-shop	la tienda de artículos de bricolaje	*lah tyehndah deh ahrteekoolohs deh breekohlaheh*
dizzy	mareado	*mahrehahdoh*

do (verb)	hacer	*ahthehr*
doctor	el médico	*ehl mehdeekoh*
dog	el perro	*ehl pehrroh*
doll	la muñeca	*lah moonyehkah*
domestic	nacionales	*nahtheeohnahlehs*
done	hecho	*ehchoh*
door	la puerta	*lah pwehrtah*
double	doble	*dohbleh*
down	abajo	*ahbah<u>h</u>oh*
draught (to be a)	haber corriente	*ahbehr kohrryehnteh*
draughts (play)	jugar a las damas	*<u>h</u>oogahr ah lahs dahmahs*
dream	soñar	*sohnyahr*
dress	el vestido	*ehl behsteedoh*
dressing gown	la bata	*lah bahtah*
drink (verb)	beber	*behbehr*
drinking chocolate	el chocolate	*ehl chohkohlahteh*
drinking water	el agua potable	*ehl ahgwah pohtahbleh*
drive (verb)	ir en coche	*eer ehn kohcheh*
driver	el chófer	*ehl chohfehr*
driving licence	el permiso de conducir	*ehl pehrmeesoh deh kohndootheer*
drought	la sequía	*lah sehkeeah*
dry (verb)	secar	*sehkahr*
dry	seco	*sehkoh*
dry clean	lavar en seco	*lahbahr ehn sehkoh*
dry cleaner's	la tintorería	*lah teentohrehreeah*
dry shampoo	el champú seco	*ehl chahmpoo sehkoh*
dummy	el chupete	*ehl choopehteh*
during	durante	*doorahnteh*
during the day	de día	*deh deeah*

E

ear	la oreja	*lah ohreh<u>h</u>ah*
ear, nose and throat (ENT) specialist	el médico de oídos	*ehl mehdeekoh deh oheedohs*
earache	el dolor de oído	*ehl dohlohr deh oheedoh*
eardrops	las gotas para los oídos	*lahs gohtahs pahrah lohs oheedohs*
early	temprano	*tehmprahnoh*
earrings	los pendientes	*lohs pehndyehntehs*
earth	la tierra	*lah tyehrrah*
earthenware	la cerámica	*lah thehrahmeekah*
east	el este	*ehl ehsteh*
easy	fácil	*fahtheel*
eat	comer	*kohmehr*
eczema	el eczema	*ehl ehkthehmah*
eel	la anguila	*lah ahngeelah*
egg	el huevo	*ehl wehboh*
elastic band	la goma elástica	*lah gohmah ehlahsteekah*
electric	eléctrico	*ehlehktreekoh*
electricity	la corriente	*lah kohrryehnteh*
embassy	la embajada	*lah ehmbah<u>h</u>ahdah*
emergency brake	el freno de emergencia	*ehl frehnoh deh ehmehr<u>h</u>ehnthyah*

English	Spanish	Pronunciation
emergency exit	la salida de emergencia	lah sahleedah deh ehmehr<u>h</u>ehnthyah
emergency number	el número de urgencias	ehl noomehroh deh oor<u>h</u>ehnthyahs
emergency phone	el teléfono de emergencia	ehl tehlehfohnoh deh ehmehr<u>h</u>ehnthyah
emergency triangle	el triángulo reflectante	ehl treeahngooloh rehflehktahnteh
emery board	la lima (para uñas)	lah leemah (pahrah oonyahs)
empty	vacío	bahtheeoh
engaged (phone)	comunicando	kohmooneekahndoh
engaged	ocupado	ohkoopahdoh
English	inglés	eenglehs
enjoy	disfrutar	deesfrootahr
entertainment guide	la guía de los espectáculos	lah gheeah deh lohs ehspehktahkoolohs
envelope	el sobre	ehl sohbreh
escort	el/la acompañante	ehl/lah ahkohmpahnyahnteh
evening	la tarde	lah tahrdeh
evening wear	el traje de etiqueta	ehl trah<u>h</u>eh deh ehteekehtah
event	el acontecimiento	ehl akohntehtheemyehntoh
event (social)	la función	lah foonthyohn
everything	todo	tohdoh
everywhere	en todas partes	ehn tohdahs pahrtehs
examine	reconocer	rehkohnohthehr
excavation	las excavaciones	lahs ehxkahbahthyohnehs
excellent	excelente, estupendo	ehxthehlehnteh, ehstoopehndoh
exchange (verb)	cambiar	kahmbyahr
exchange office	la oficina de cambio	lah ohfeetheenah deh kahmbyoh
exchange rate	la cotización, el tipo de cambio	lah kohteethahthyohn, ehl teepoh deh kahmbyoh
excursion	la excursión organizada	lah ehxkoorsyohn ohrgahneethahdah
exhibition	la exposición	lah ehxpohseethyohn
exit	la salida	lah sahleedah
expenses	los gastos	lohs gahstohs
expensive	caro	kahroh
explain	explicar	ehxpleekahr
express train	el tren rápido	ehl trehn rahpeedoh
external	tópico, externo	tohpeekoh, ehxtehrnoh
eye	el ojo	ehl oh<u>h</u>oh
eye drops	las gotas para los ojos	lahs gohtahs pahrah lohs oh<u>h</u>ohs
eye shadow	la sombra de ojos	lah sohmbrah deh oh<u>h</u>ohs
eye specialist	el oculista	ehl ohkooleestah
eyeliner	el lápiz de ojos	ehl lahpeeth deh oh<u>h</u>ohs

F

English	Spanish	Pronunciation
face	la cara	*lah kahrah*
factory	la fábrica	*lah fahbreekah*
fair	la feria	*lah fehryah*
fall	caer(se)	*kahehr(seh)*
family	la familia	*lah fahmeelyah*
famous	famoso	*fahmohsoh*
far away	lejos	*leh<u>h</u>ohs*
farm	la granja	*lah grahn<u>h</u>ah*
farmer	el campesino	*ehl kahmpehseenoh*
farmer's wife	la campesina	*lah kahmpehseenah*
fashion	la moda	*lah mohdah*
fast	rápido	*rahpeedoh*
father	el padre	*ehl pahdreh*
fault (blame)	la culpa	*lah koolpah*
fax (verb)	enviar un fax	*ehnbyahr oon fahx*
February	febrero	*fehbrehroh*
feel (verb)	sentir	*sehnteer*
feel like	apetecer	*ahpehtehthehr*
fence	la verja	*lah behr<u>h</u>ah*
ferry	el transbordador	*ehl trahnsbohrdahdohr*
fever	la fiebre	*lah fyehbreh*
fill (tooth)	empastar	*ehmpahstahr*
fill out	rellenar	*rehlyehnahr*
filling	el empaste	*ehl ehmpahsteh*
film (camera)	el rollo	*ehl rohlyoh*
film	la película	*lah pehleekoolah*
filter	el filtro	*ehl feeltroh*
find (verb)	encontrar	*ehnkohntrahr*
fine	la multa	*lah mooltah*
finger	el dedo	*ehl dehdoh*
fire	el fuego	*ehl fwehgoh*
fire (house etc.)	el incendio	*ehl eenthehndyoh*
fire brigade	los bomberos	*lohs bohmbehrohs*
fire escape	la escalera de incendios	*lah ehskahlehrah deh eenthehndyohs*
fire extinguisher	el extintor	*ehl ehxteentohr*
first	primero	*preemehroh*
first aid	los primeros auxilios	*lohs preemehrohs ahooxeelyohs*
first class	la primera clase	*lah preemehrah klahseh*
fish (verb)	pescar	*pehskahr*
fish	el pescado	*ehl pehskahdoh*
fishing rod	la caña de pescar	*lah kanyah deh pehskahr*
fitness centre	el gimnasio	*ehl <u>h</u>eemnahsyoh*
fitness training	la gimnasia	*lah <u>h</u>eemnahsyah*
fitting room	el probador	*ehl prohbahdohr*
fix puncture	arreglar el pinchazo	*ahrrehglahr ehl peenchahthoh*
flag	la bandera	*lah bahndehrah*
flamenco	el flamenco	*ehl flahmehnkoh*
flash cube	el cuboflash	*ehl koobohflahsh*
flash gun/bulb	el flash	*ehl flahsh*
flat	el piso	*ehl peesoh*

Word list

15

flea market	el mercadillo, el rastro	_ehl mehrkahdeelyoh, ehl rahstroh_
flight	el vuelo	_ehl bwehloh_
flight number	el número de vuelo	_ehl noomehroh deh bwehloh_
flood	la inundación	_lah eenoondathyohn_
floor	el piso	_ehl peesoh_
flour	la harina	_lah ahreenah_
flu	la gripe	_lah greepeh_
fly (insect)	la mosca	_lah mohskah_
fly (verb)	volar	_bohlahr_
fly-over	el viaducto	_ehl beeahdooktoh_
fog	la niebla	_lah nyehblah_
foggy (be)	haber niebla	_ahbehr nyehblah_
folkloristic	folclórico	_fohlklohreekoh_
follow	seguir	_sehgeer_
food	el alimento	_ehl ahleemehntoh_
food poisoning	la intoxicación alimenticia	_lah eentohxeekaht-hyohn ahleemehntee-thyah_
foodstuffs	los víveres	_lohs beebehrehs_
foot	el pie	_ehl pyeh_
for	antes, delante de	_ahntehs, dehlahnteh deh_
for hire	se alquila	_seh ahlkeelah_
forbidden	prohibido	_proheebeedoh_
forehead	la frente	_lah frehnteh_
foreign	extranjero	_ehxtrahn<u>h</u>ehroh_
forget	olvidar	_ohlbeedahr_
fork	el tenedor	_ehl tehnehdohr_
form	el formulario	_ehl fohrmoolahryoh_
fort	la fortificación	_lah fohrteefeekah-thyohn_
forward (send)	enviar	_ehnbyahr_
fountain	la fuente	_lah fwehnteh_
four-star petrol	súper	_soopehr_
frame	la montura	_lah mohntoorah_
free	libre	_leebreh_
free of charge	gratuito	_grahtweetoh_
free time	el tiempo libre	_ehl tyehmpoh leebreh_
freeze	helar	_ehlahr_
French	francés	_frahnthehs_
French bread	la barra de pan	_lah bahrrah deh pahn_
fresh	fresco	_frehskoh_
Friday	el viernes	_ehl byehrnehs_
fried	frito	_freetoh_
fried egg	el huevo al plato	_ehl wehboh ahl plahtoh_
friend	el amigo	_ehl ahmeegoh_
friendly	cordial, amable	_kohrdyahl, ahmahbleh_
frightened	miedoso	_myehdohsoh_
fringe	el flequillo	_ehl flehkeelyoh_
front (at the)	adelante	_ahdehlahnteh_
frozen goods	los productos congelados	_los prohdooktohs kohn<u>h</u>ehlahdohs_
fruit	la fruta	_lah frootah_
fruit juice	el zumo de frutas	_ehl thoomoh deh frootahs_

English	Spanish	Pronunciation
frying pan	la sartén	*lah sahrtehn*
full	lleno	*lyehnoh*
fun	la diversión	*lah deebehrsyohn*

G

gallery	la galería de arte	*lah gahlehreeah deh ahrteh*
game	el juego	*el hwehgoh*
garage (for repairs)	el taller mecánico	*ehl tahlyehr mehkahneekoh*
garbage bag	la bolsa de basura	*lah bohlsah deh bahsoorah*
garden	el jardín	*ehl hahrdeen*
gastroenteritis	la gastroenteritis	*lah gahstrohehnteh-reetees*
gauze	la gasa esterilizada	*lah gahsah ehstehreeleethahdah*
gear (bicycle)	el cambio	*ehl kahmbyoh*
gel	el gel	*ehl hehl*
German	alemán	*ahlehmahn*
get married	casarse	*kahsahrseh*
get off	bajarse	*bahhahrse*
gift	el regalo	*ehl rehgahloh*
gilt	dorado	*dohrahdoh*
ginger	el jengibre	*ehl hehnheebreh*
girl	la chica	*lah cheekah*
girlfriend	la amiga	*lah ahmeegah*
giro card	la tarjeta de la caja postal	*lah tahrhehtah deh lah kahhah pohstahl*
giro cheque	el cheque postal	*ehl chehkeh pohstahl*
glacier	el glaciar	*ehl glahthyahr*
glass (tumbler)	el vaso	*ehl bahsoh*
glass (wine -)	la copa	*lah kohpah*
glasses	las gafas	*lahs gahfahs*
glider	el vuelo sin motor	*ehl bwehloh seen mohtohr*
glove	el guante	*ehl gwahnteh*
glue	la cola	*lah kohlah*
gnat	el mosquito	*ehl mohskeetoh*
go (verb)	ir	*eer*
go back, come back	volver	*bohlbehr*
go backwards	ir para atrás	*eer pahrah ahtrahs*
go out	salir	*sahleer*
goat's cheese	el queso de cabra	*ehl kehsoh deh kahbrah*
gold	el oro	*ehl ohroh*
golf	el golf	*ehl gohlf*
golf course	el campo de golf	*ehl kahmpoh deh gohlf*
gone	perdido	*pehrdeedoh*
good afternoon	buenas tardes (after 2pm)	*bwehnahs tahrdehs*
good evening	buenas tardes	*bwehnahs tahrdehs*
good morning	buenos días (before 2pm)	*bwehnohs deeahs*
good night	buenas noches	*bwehnahs nohchehs*
goodbye	la despedida	*lah dehspehdeedah*
gram	el gramo	*ehl grahmoh*
grandchild	el nieto	*ehl nyehtoh*

grandfather	el abuelo	*ehl ahbwehloh*
grandmother	la abuela	*lah ahbwehlah*
grape juice	el zumo de uvas	*ehl thoomoh deh oobahs*
grapefruit	el pomelo	*ehl pohmehloh*
grapes	las uvas	*lahs oobahs*
grave	la tumba	*lah toombah*
grease	la grasa	*lah grahsah*
green	verde	*behrdeh*
green card	la tarjeta verde	*lah tahrhehtah behrdeh*
greet	saludar	*sahloodahr*
grey (hair)	canoso	*kahnohsoh*
grey	gris	*grees*
grill (verb)	asar a la parrilla	*ahsahr ah lah pahreelyah*
grilled	tostado	*tohstahdoh*
grocer's	la tienda de comestibles	*lah tyehndah deh kohmehsteeblehs*
ground	la tierra	*lah tyehrrah*
group	el grupo	*ehl groopoh*
guest house	la pensión	*lah pehnsyohn*
guide (book)	la guía	*lah gueeah*
guide (person)	el/la guía	*ehl/lah gueeah*
guided tour	la visita guiada	*lah beeseetah gueeahdah*
gynaecologist	el ginecólogo	*ehl heenehkohlohgoh*

H

hair	el pelo	*ehl pehloh*
hairbrush	el cepillo para el pelo	*ehl thehpeelyoh parah ehl pehloh*
hairdresser (ladies', men's)	la peluquería (de señoras, caballeros)	*lah pehlookehreeah (deh sehnyohrahs, kahbahlyehrohs)*
hairpins	las horquillas	*lahs ohrkeelyahs*
hairspray	la laca para el pelo	*lah lahkah pahrah ehl pehloh*
half	medio, media, la mitad	*mehdyoh, mehdyah, lah meetahdh*
half full	lleno hasta la mitad	*lyehnoh ahstah lah meetahdh*
half kilo	el medio kilo	*ehl mehdyoh keeloh*
hammer	el martillo	*ehl mahrteelyoh*
hand	la mano	*lah mahnoh*
hand brake	el freno de mano	*ehl frehnoh deh mahnoh*
handbag	el bolso de mano	*ehl bohlsoh deh mahnoh*
handbag	el bolso	*ehl bohlsoh*
handkerchief	el pañuelo	*ehl pahnywehloh*
handmade	hecho a mano	*ehchoh ah mahnoh*
happy	contento	*kohntehntoh*
harbour	el puerto	*ehl pwehrtoh*
hard	duro	*dooroh*
haste	la prisa	*lah preesah*
hat	el sombrero	*ehl sohmbrehroh*

hay fever	la fiebre del heno	*lah fyehbreh dehl ehnoh*
hazelnut	la avellana	*lah ahbehlyahnah*
head	la cabeza	*lah kahbehthah*
headache	el dolor de cabeza	*ehl dohlohr deh kahbehthah*
health	la salud	*lah sahloodh*
health food shop	la tienda naturista	*lah tyehndah nahtooreestah*
hear	entender	*ehntehndehr*
hearing aid	el audífono	*ehl ahoodeefohnoh*
heart	el corazón	*ehl kohrahthohn*
heart patient	el enfermo cardíaco	*ehl ehnfehrmoh kahrdeeahkoh*
heat	calor	*kahlohr*
heater	la calefacción	*lah kahlehfahkthyohn*
heavy	pesado	*pehsahdoh*
heel	el talón	*ehl tahlohn*
heel (on shoe)	el tacón	*ehl tahkohn*
hello	hola	*ohlah*
helmet	el casco	*ehl kahskoh*
help (verb)	ayudar	*ahyoodahr*
help	la ayuda	*lah ahyoodah*
helping/portion	la ración	*lah rahthyohn*
herbal tea	la infusión	*lah eenfoosyohn*
here	aquí	*ahkee*
herring	el arenque	*ehl ahrehnkeh*
high	alto	*ahltoh*
high tide	la marea alta	*lah mahrehah ahltah*
highchair	la silla para niños	*lah seelyah pahrah neenyohs*
hiking	el excursionismo	*ehl ehxkoorsyohneesmoh*
hiking trip	la excursión a pie	*lah ehxkoorsyohn ah pyeh*
hip	la cadera	*lah kahdehrah*
hire	alquilar	*ahlkeelahr*
hitchhike	hacer autostop	*ahthehr ahootohstohp*
hobby	el hobby	*ehl hohbee*
hold-up/robbery	el asalto	*ehl ahsahltoh*
holiday (public)	el día de fiesta	*ehl deeah deh fyehstah*
holiday house	el chalet	*ehl chahleh*
holiday park	la urbanización	*lah oorbahneethah-thyohn*
holidays	las vacaciones	*lahs bahkahthyohnehs*
home (at)	en casa	*ehn kahsah*
homesickness	la nostalgia	*lah nohstahl<u>h</u>yah*
honest	sincero	*seenthehroh*
honey	la miel	*lah myehl*
horizontal	horizontal	*oreethohntahl*
horrible	horrible	*ohrreebleh*
horse	el caballo	*ehl kahbahlyoh*
hospital	el hospital	*ehl ohspeetahl*
hospitality	la hospitalidad	*lah ohspeetahleedahdh*
hot	cálido/caluroso	*kahleedoh/kahloorohsoh*
hot (spicy)	picante	*peekahnteh*

Word list

15

hotel	el hotel	*ehl ohtehl*
hot-water bottle	la bolsa de agua caliente	*lah bohlsah deh ahgwah kahlyehnteh*
hour	la hora	*lah ohrah*
house	la casa	*lah kahsah*
household items	los artículos del hogar	*lohs ahrteekoolohs dehl ohgahr*
houses of parliament	la cámara de diputados	*lah kahmahrah deh deepootahdohs*
housewife	el ama de casa	*ehl ahmah deh kahsah*
how far?	¿a qué distancia?	*ah keh deestahnthyah?*
how long?	¿cuánto tiempo?	*kwahntoh tyehmpoh?*
how much?	¿cuánto?	*kwahntoh?*
how?	¿cómo?	*kohmoh*
hunger	el hambre/el apetito	*ehl ahmbreh/ehl ahpehteetoh*
hurricane	el huracán	*ehl oorahkahn*
hurry	la prisa	*lah preesah*
husband	el marido	*ehl mahreedoh*
hut	el camarote	*ehl kahmahrohteh*
hyperventilation	la hiperventilación	*lah eepehr-behnteelahthyohn*

I

ice cream	el helado	*ehl ehlahdoh*
ice cubes	los cubitos de hielo	*lohs koobeetohs deh yehloh*
ice skating	el patinaje sobre hielo	*ehl pahteenahheh sohbreh yehloh*
idea	la idea	*lah eedehah*
identification card	el carnet de identidad	*ehl kahrneh deh eedehnteedahdh*
identify	identificar	*eedehnteefeekahr*
ignition key	la llave de contacto	*lah lyahbeh deh kohntahktoh*
ill	enfermo	*ehnfehrmoh*
illness	la enfermedad	*lah ehnfehrmehdahdh*
imagine	imaginarse	*eemahheenahrseh*
immediately	inmediatamente	*eenmehdyahtah-mehnteh*
import duty	los derechos de aduana	*lohs dehrehchohs deh ahdwahnah*
impossible	imposible	*eempohseebleh*
in	en	*ehn*
in the evening	por la tarde	*pohr lah tahrdeh*
in the morning	por la mañana	*pohr lah mahnyahnah*
included	incluido	*eenklooeedoh*
indicate	señalar	*sehnyahlahr*
indicator	el intermitente	*ehl eentehrmeeteenteh*
inexpensive	barato	*bahrahtoh*
infection (viral -, bacterial -)	la infección (vírica, bacteriana)	*lah eenfehkthyohn (beereekah, bahktehryahnah)*
inflammation	la inflamación	*lah eenflahmahthyohn*
information	la información	*lah eenfohrmahthyohn*
information office	la oficina de información	*lah ohfeetheenah deh eenfohrmahthyohn*

injection	la inyección	*lah eenyehkthyohn*
injured	herido	*erhreedoh*
inner ear	el oído	*ehl oheedoh*
inner tube	la cámara	*lah kahmahrah*
innocent	inocente	*eenohthehnte*
insect	el insecto	*ehl eensehktoh*
insect bite	la picadura de insecto	*lah peekahdoorah deh eensehktoh*
insect repellant	el aceite para los mosquitos	*ehl ahthehyteh pahrah lohs mohskeetohs*
inside	adentro	*ahdehntroh*
insole	la plantilla	*lah plahnteelyah*
instructions	las instrucciones	*lahs eenstrookthyohnehs*
insurance	el seguro	*ehl sehgooroh*
intermission	la pausa	*lah pahoosah*
international	internacional	*eentehrnahthyohnahl*
interpreter	el intérprete	*ehl eentehrprehteh*
intersection/crossing	el cruce	*ehl kreeotheh*
introduce oneself	presentarse	*prehsehntahrseh*
invite (verb)	invitar	*eenbeetahr*
iodine	el yodo	*ehl yohdoh*
iron (metal)	el hierro	*ehl yehrroh*
iron (verb)	planchar	*plahnchahr*
iron	la plancha	*lah plahnchah*
ironing board	la tabla de planchar	*lah tahblah deh plahnchahr*
island	la isla	*lah eeslah*
it's a pleasure	de nada	*deh nahdah*
Italian	italiano	*eetahlyahnoh*
itch	la picazón	*lah peekahthohn*

J

jack	el gato	*ehl gahtoh*
jacket	la chaqueta	*lah chahkehtah*
jam	la mermelada	*lah mehrmehlahdah*
January	enero	*ehnehroh*
jaw	la mandíbula	*lah mahndeeboolah*
jellyfish	la medusa	*lah mehdoosah*
jeweller	la joyería	*lah hoyehreeah*
jewels	las alhajas	*lahs ahlahhahs*
jog (verb)	hacer footing	*ahthehr footeen*
joke	la broma	*lah brohmah*
journey	el viaje	*ehl byahheh*
juice	el zumo/el jugo	*ehl thoomoh/ehl hoogoh*
July	julio	*hoolyoh*
jump leads	el cable de arranque	*ehl kahbleh deh ahrrahnkeh*
jumper	el jersey	*ehl hehrsehee*
June	junio	*hoonyoh*

K

key	la llave	*lah lyahbeh*
kilo	el kilo	*ehl keeloh*
kilometre	kilómetro(s)	*keelohmehtroh(s)*
king	el rey	*ehl rehee*

kiss (verb)	besar	*behsahr*
kiss	el beso	*ehl behsoh*
kitchen	la cocina	*lah kohtheenah*
knee	la rodilla	*lah rohdeelyah*
knee socks	las medias cortas	*lahs mehdyahs kohrtahs*
knife	el cuchillo	*ehl koocheelyoh*
know	saber	*sahbehr*

L

lace	el encaje	*ehl ehnkah<u>h</u>eh*
ladies'	el servicio para señoras	*ehl sehrbeethyoh pahrah sehnyohrahs*
lake	el lago	*ehl lahgoh*
lamp	la lámpara	*lah lahmpahrah*
land (verb)	aterrizar	*ahtehrreethahr*
lane	el carril	*ehl kahrreel*
language	el idioma	*ehl eedyohmah*
large	grande	*grahndeh*
last	pasado, último	*pahsahdoh, oolteemoh*
last night	anoche	*ahnohcheh*
late	tarde	*tahrdeh*
later	luego	*lwehgoh*
latest (at the)	a más tardar	*ah mahs tahrdahr*
laugh	reír	*reheer*
launderette	la lavandería (automática)	*lah lahbahndehreeah (ahootohmahteekah)*
law	el derecho	*ehl dehrehchoh*
laxative	el laxante	*ehl lahxahnteh*
leak	pinchado	*peenchahdoh*
leather	la piel, el cuero	*lah pyehl, ehl kwehroh*
leather goods	los artículos de piel	*lohs ahrteekoolohs deh pyehl*
leave (verb)	partir, salir	*pahrteer, sahleer*
leek	el puerro	*ehl pwehrroh*
left (on the)	a la izquierda	*ah lah eethkyehrdah*
left	izquierda	*eethkyehrdah*
left luggage	el depósito de equipajes	*ehl dehpohseetoh deh ehkeepah<u>h</u>ehs*
leg	la pierna	*lah pyehrnah*
lemon	el limón	*ehl leemohn*
lemonade	la limonada	*lah leemohnahdah*
lend	prestar	*prehstahr*
lens	el objetivo	*ehl ohb<u>h</u>ehteeboh*
lentils	las lentejas	*lahs lehnteh<u>h</u>ahs*
less	menos	*mehnohs*
lesson	la clase	*lah klahseh*
letter	la carta	*lah kahrtah*
lettuce	la lechuga	*lah lehchoogah*
level crossing	el paso a nivel	*ehl pahsoh ah neebehl*
library	la biblioteca	*lah beeblyohtehkah*
lie	mentir	*mehnteer*
lie down	estar tumbado	*ehstahr toombahdoh*
lift (hitchhike)	el viaje (en autostop)	*ehl byah<u>h</u>eh (ehn ahootohstohp)*
lift (in building)	el ascensor	*ehl ahsthehnsohr*

Word list

15

lift (ski)	el telesquí, el telesilla	*ehl tehlehskee,ehl tehlehseelyah*
light (for cigarette)	el fuego	*ehl fwehgoh*
light (not dark)	claro	*klahroh*
light (not heavy)	ligero	*leehehroh*
lighter	el mechero	*ehl mehchehroh*
lighthouse	el faro	*ehl fahroh*
lightning	el rayo	*ehl rahyoh*
like	gustar	*goostahr*
line	la línea	*lah leenehah*
linen	el hilo	*ehl eeloh*
lipstick	la barra de labios	*lah bahrrah deh lahbyohs*
liqueur	la copa	*lah kohpah*
liquorice	el regaliz	*ehl rehgahleeth*
listen	escuchar	*ehskoochahr*
literature	la literatura	*lah leetehrahtoorah*
litre	el litro	*ehl leetroh*
little	poco	*pohkoh*
live (verb)	vivir	*beebeer*
live together	vivir con otra persona	*beebeer kohn ohtrah pehrsohnah*
lobster	la langosta	*lah lahngohstah*
local	local	*lohkahl*
lock	la cerradura	*lah thehrrahdoorah*
long	largo	*lahrgoh*
look (verb)	mirar	*meerahr*
look for	buscar	*booskahr*
look up (person)	buscar	*booskahr*
lorry	el camión	*ehl kahmyohn*
lose	perder	*pehrdehr*
loss	la pérdida	*lah pehrdeedah*
lost (to get)	perderse, extraviarse	*pehrdehrse, ehxtrahbyahrseh*
lost	extraviado, perdido	*ehxtrahbyahdoh, pehrdeedoh*
lost item	extravío	*ehxtrahbeeoh*
lost property office	los objetos perdidos	*lohs ohbhehtohs pehrdeedohs*
lotion	la loción	*lah lohthyohn*
loud	alto	*ahltoh*
love (be in - with)	estar enamorado de	*ehstahr ehnahmohrahdoh deh*
love (verb)	querer	*kehrehr*
love	el amor	*ehl ahmohr*
low	bajo	*bahhoh*
low tide	la marea baja	*lah mahrehah bahhah*
luck	la suerte	*lah swehrteh*
luggage	el equipaje	*ehl ehkeepahheh*
luggage locker	la consigna automática	*lah kohnseegnah ahootohmahteekah*
lunch	el almuerzo, la comida	*ehl ahlmwehrthoh, lah kohmeedah*
lungs	los pulmones	*lohs poolmohnehs*

Word list

15

musical show	la comedia musical	*lah kohmehdyah mooseekahl*
mussels	los mejillones	*lohs meheelyohnehs*
mustard	la mostaza	*lah mohstahthah*

N

nail (on hand)	la uña	*lah oonyah*
nail	el clavo	*ehl klahboh*
nail polish	el esmalte (para uñas)	*ehl ehsmahlteh(pahrah oonyahs)*
nail polish remover	el quitaesmalte	*ehl keetahehsmahlteh*
nail scissors	las tijeras de uñas	*lahs tee<u>h</u>ehrahs pahrah oonyahs*
naked	desnudo	*dehsnoodoh*
nappy	el pañal	*ehl pahnyahl*
nationality	la nacionalidad	*lah nahthyohnahlee-dahdh*
nature	la naturaleza	*lah nahtoorahlehthah*
naturism	el naturismo	*ehl nahtooreesmoh*
nauseous	con náuseas	*kohn nahoosehahs*
near	junto a	*<u>h</u>oontoh ah*
nearby	cerca	*thehrkah*
necessary	necesario	*nehthehsahryoh*
neck	la nuca	*lah nookah*
necklace	la cadena	*lah kahdehnah*
needle	la aguja	*lah ahoo<u>h</u>ah*
negative	el negativo	*ehl nehgahteeboh*
neighbours	los vecinos	*lohs behtheenohs*
nephew	el sobrino	*ehl sohbreenoh*
Netherlands	los Países Bajos	*lohs paheesehs bah<u>h</u>ohs*
never	jamás/nunca	*<u>h</u>ahmahs/noonkah*
new	nuevo	*nwehboh*
news	las noticias	*lahs nohteethyahs*
news stand	el quiosco	*ehl kyohskoh*
newspaper	el periódico	*ehl pehryohdeekoh*
next	próximo, que viene	*prohxeemoh, keh byehneh*
next to	al lado de	*ahl lahdoh deh*
nice (friendly)	amable	*ahmahbleh*
nice (to look at)	bonito, mono	*bohneetoh, mohnoh*
nice	bien, agradable	*byehn, ahgrahdahbleh*
niece	la sobrina	*lah sohbreenah*
night (at)	por la noche	*pohr lah nohcheh*
night	la noche	*lah nohcheh*
night duty	la guardia nocturna	*lah gwahrdyah nohktoornah*
nightclub	el cabaré	*ehl kahbahreh*
nightlife	la vida nocturna	*lah beedah nohktoornah*
nipple	la tetina	*lah tehteenah*
no	no	*noh*
no overtaking	la prohibición de adelantar	*lah proheebeethyohn deh ahdehlahntahr*
noise	el ruido	*ehl rooeedoh*
nonstop	sin escalas	*seen ehskahlahs*
no-one	nadie	*nahdyeh*

normal	normal, corriente	*nohrmahl, kohrryehnteh*
north	el norte	*ehl nohrteh*
nose	la nariz	*lah nahreeth*
nose bleed	la hemorragia nasal	*lah ehmohrrah<u>h</u>yah nahsahl*
nose drops	las gotas para la nariz	*lahs gohtahs pahrah lah nahreeth*
notepaper	el papel de escribir	*ehl pahpehl deh ehskreebeer*
nothing	nada	*nahdah*
November	noviembre	*nohbyehmbreh*
nowhere	en ninguna parte	*ehn neengoonah pahrteh*
nudist beach	la playa nudista	*lah plahyah noodeestah*
number	el número	*ehl noomehroh*
number plate	la matrícula	*lah mahtreekoolah*
nurse	la enfermera	*lah ehnfehrmehrah*
nutmeg	la nuez moscada	*lah nwehth mohskahdah*
nuts	los frutos secos	*lohs frootohs sehkohs*

O

October	octubre	*ohktoobreh*
of course	claro	*klahroh*
off	podrido	*pohdreedoh*
offer	ofrecer	*ohfrehthehr*
office	la oficina	*lah ohfeetheenah*
off-licence	la bodega, la tienda de vinos y licores	*lah bohdehgah, lah tyehndah deh beenohs ee leekohrehs*
oil	el aceite	*ehl ahtheyteh*
oil level	el nivel del aceite	*ehl neebehl deh ahtheyteh*
ointment	la pomada, el ungüento	*lah pohmahdah, ehl oongwehntoh*
ointment for burns	la pomada contra las quemaduras	*lah pohmahdah kohntrah lahs kehmahdoorahs*
okay	vale, de acuerdo	*bahleh, deh ahkwehrdoh*
old	viejo	*byeh<u>h</u>oh*
old part of town	el casco antiguo	*ehl kahskoh ahnteegwoh*
olive oil	el aceite de oliva	*ehl ahtheyteh deh ohleebah*
olives	las aceitunas	*lahs ahtheytoonahs*
omelette	la tortilla	*lah tohrteelyah*
on	sobre	*sohbreh*
on board	a bordo	*ah bohrdoh*
oncoming car	el vehículo que viene	*ehl beheekooloh keh byehneh*
one hundred grams	los cien gramos	*lohs thyehn grahmohs*
one-way traffic	la dirección única	*lah deerehkthyohn ooneekah*
onion	la cebolla	*lah thehbohlyah*
open (adj.)	abierto	*ahbyehrtoh*
open (verb)	abrir	*ahbreer*

opera	la ópera	*lah ohpehrah*
operate	operar	*ohpehrahr*
operator (telephone)	la operadora	*lah ohpehrahdohrah*
operetta	la opereta, la zarzuela	*lah ohpehrehtah, lah thahrthwehlah*
opposite	al frente, enfrente de	*ahl frehnteh, ehnfrehnteh deh*
optician	la óptica	*lah ohpteekah*
orange	la naranja	*lah nahrah<u>nh</u>ah*
orange (adj.)	naranja	*nahrah<u>nh</u>ah*
orange juice	el zumo de naranja	*ehl thoomoh deh nahrah<u>nh</u>ah*
order (in -,) tidy	en orden, ordenado	*ehn ohrdehn, ohrdehnahdo*
order (verb)	pedir	*pehdeer*
order	el pedido	*ehl pehdeedoh*
other	otro	*ohtroh*
other side	el otro lado	*ehl ohtroh lahdoh*
outside	afuera	*ahfwehrah*
overtake	adelantar	*ahdehlahntahr*
oysters	las ostras	*lahs ohstrahs*

P

packed lunch	el paquete con bocadillos	*ehl pahkehteh kohn bohkahdeelyohs*
page	la página	*lah pah<u>h</u>eenah*
pain	el dolor	*ehl dohlohr*
painkiller	el analgésico	*ehl ahnahl<u>h</u>ehseekoh*
paint (verb)	pintar	*peentahr*
paint	la pintura	*lah peentoorah*
painting (art)	el cuadro	*ehl kwahdroh*
painting (object)	la pintura	*lah peentoorah*
palace	el palacio	*ehl pahlahthyoh*
pancake	la crepe	*lah krehp*
pane	el cristal	*ehl kreestahl*
pants (briefs)	las bragas	*lahs brahgahs*
panty liner	el protegeslip	*ehl prohteh<u>h</u>ehsleep*
paper	el papel	*ehl pahpehl*
paraffin oil	el querosén	*ehl kehrohsehn*
parasol	el quitasol	*ehl keetahsohl*
parcel	el paquete	*ehl pahkehteh*
pardon	perdone	*pehrdohneh*
parents	los padres	*lohs pahdrehs*
park	el parque	*ehl pahrkeh*
park (verb)	aparcar	*ahpahrkahr*
parking space	el sitio para aparcar	*ehl seetyoh pahrah ahpahrkahr*
parsley	el perejil	*ehl pehreh<u>h</u>eel*
partition	la secreción	*lah sehkrehthyohn*
partner	la pareja	*lah pahreh<u>h</u>ah*
party	la fiesta	*lah fyehstah*
passable	practicable	*prahkteekahbleh*
passenger	el pasajero	*ehl pahsah<u>h</u>ehroh*
passport	el pasaporte	*ehl pahsahpohrteh*
passport photo	la foto de carnet	*lah fohtoh deh kahrneh*
patient	el paciente	*ehl pahthyehnteh*
pavement	la acera	*lah ahthehrah*

Word list

15

140

pay (verb)	pagar	*pahgahr*
pay the bill	pagar la cuenta	*pahgahr lah kwehntah*
peach	el melocotón	*ehl mehlohkohtohn*
peanuts	los cacahuetes	*lohs kahkahwehtehs*
pear	la pera	*lah pehrah*
peas	los guisantes	*lohs gueesahntehs*
pedal	el pedal	*ehl pehdahl*
pedestrian crossing	el paso de peatones	*ehl pahsoh deh pehahtohnehs*
pedicure	la pedicura	*lah pehdeekoorah*
pen	la pluma	*lah ploomah*
pencil (hard/soft)	el lápiz (duro/blando)	*ehl lahpeeth (dooroh /blahndoh)*
penis	el pene	*ehl pehneh*
pepper (capsicum)	el pimiento	*ehl peemyehntoh*
pepper (condiment)	la pimienta	*lah peemyehntah*
performance	la función de teatro /música	*lah foonthyohn deh tehahtroh/mooseekah*
perfume	el perfume	*ehl pehrfoomeh*
perm (verb)	hacer una permanente	*ahthehr oonah pehrmahnehnteh*
perm	la permanente	*lah pehrmahnehnteh*
permit	el permiso	*ehl pehrmeesoh*
person	la persona	*lah pehrsohnah*
personal	personal	*pehrsohnahl*
petrol	la gasolina	*lah gahsohleenah*
petrol station	la gasolinera	*lah gahsohleenehrah*
pets	los animales domésticos	*lohs ahneemahles dohmehsteekohs*
pharmacy	la farmacia	*lah fahrmahthyah*
phone (by)	por teléfono	*pohr tehlehfohnoh*
phone (tele-)	el teléfono	*ehl tehlehfohnoh*
phone (verb)	llamar por teléfono	*lyahmahr pohr tehlehfohnoh*
phone box	la cabina telefónica	*lah kahbeenah tehlehfohneekah*
phone directory	la guía de teléfonos	*lah gheeah deh tehlehfohnohs*
phone number	el número de teléfono	*ehl noomehroh deh tehlehfohnoh*
photo	la foto	*lah fohtoh*
photocopier	la fotocopiadora	*lah fohtohkohpyahdohrah*
photocopy (verb)	fotocopiar	*fohtohkohpyahr*
photocopy	la fotocopia	*lah fohtohkohpyah*
pick up (fetch person)	(ir a) buscar, pasar a buscar	*(eer ah) booskahr, pahsahr ah booskahr*
picnic	el picnic	*ehl peekneek*
piece of clothing	la prenda	*lah prehndah*
pier	el muelle	*ehl mwehlyeh*
pigeon	la paloma	*lah pahlohmah*
pill (contraceptive)	la píldora (anticonceptiva)	*lah peeldohrah (ahnteekohnthehp- teebah)*
pillow	la almohada	*lah ahlmohahdah*
pillowcase	la funda de almohada	*lah foondah deh ahlmohahdah*

pin	el alfiler	*ehl ahlfeelehr*
pineapple	la piña	*lah peenyah*
pipe	la pipa	*lah peepah*
pipe tobacco	el tabaco de pipa	*ehl tahbahkoh deh peepah*
pity	lástima	*lahsteemah*
place of entertainment	el sitio para salir	*ehl seetyoh pahrah sahleer*
place of interest	el punto de interés	*ehl poontoh deh eentehrehs*
plan/map	el plano	*ehl plahnoh*
plant	la planta	*lah plahntah*
plasters	las tiritas, los esparadrapos	*lahs teereetahs, lohs ehspahrah-drahpohs*
plastic	el plástico	*ehl plahsteekoh*
plastic bag	la bolsita	*lah bohlseetah*
plate	el plato	*ehl plahtoh*
platform	la vía, el andén	*lah beeah, ehl ahndehn*
play (theatre)	la obra de teatro	*lah ohbrah deh tehahtroh*
play (verb)	jugar	*hoogahr*
playground	el parque infantil	*ehl pahrkeh eenfahnteel*
playing cards	los naipes	*lohs naypehs*
pleasant	agradable	*ahgrahdahbleh*
please	por favor	*pohr fahbohr*
pleasure	el placer	*ehl plahthehr*
plum	la ciruela	*lah theerwehlah*
pocketknife	la navaja	*lah nahbahhah*
point (verb)	indicar	*eendeekahr*
poison	el veneno	*ehl behnehnoh*
police	la policía	*lah pohleetheeah*
police station	la comisaría	*la kohmeesahreeah*
policeman	el guardia	*ehl gwahrdyah*
pond	el estanque	*ehl ehstahnkeh*
pony	el poney	*ehl pohnehy*
pop concert	el concierto pop	*ehl kohnthyehrtoh pohp*
population	la población	*lah pohblahthyohn*
pork	la carne de cerdo	*lah kahrneh deh thehrdoh*
port wine	el oporto	*ehl ohpohrtoh*
porter	el portero	*ehl pohrtehroh*
post code	el código postal	*ehl cohdeegoh pohstahl*
post office	la oficina de Correos	*lah ohfeetheenah deh cohrrehohs*
postage	el franqueo	*ehl frahnkehoh*
postbox	el buzón	*ehl boothohn*
postcard	la (tarjeta) postal	*lah (tahrhehtah) pohstahl*
postman	el cartero	*ehl kahrtehroh*
potato	la patata	*lah pahtahtah*
poultry	las aves	*lahs ahbehs*
powdered milk	la leche en polvo	*lah lehcheh ehn pohlboh*

power point	la toma de corriente	*lah tohmah deh kohrryehnteh*
pram	el cochecito	*ehl kohchehtheetoh*
prawns	las gambas	*lahs gahmbahs*
precious	querido	*kehreedoh*
prefer	preferir	*prehfehreer*
preference	la preferencia	*lah prehfehrehnthyah*
pregnant	embarazada	*ehmbahrahthahdah*
present	presente	*prehsehnteh*
present (gift)	el regalo	*ehl rehgahloh*
press (verb)	apretar	*ahprehtahr*
pressure	la tensión	*lah tehnsyohn*
price	el precio	*ehl prehthyoh*
price list	la lista de precios	*lah leestah deh prehthyohs*
print (verb)	copiar	*kohpyahr*
print	la copia	*lah kohpyah*
probably	probablemente	*prohbahblehmehnteh*
problem	el problema	*ehl prohblehmah*
profession	la profesión	*lah prohfehsyohn*
programme	el programa	*ehl prohgrahmah*
pronounce	pronunciar	*prohnoonthyahr*
propane camping gas	el gas propano	*ehl gahs prohpahnoh*
pull	sacar	*sahkahr*
pull a muscle	distender un músculo	*deestehndehr oon mooskooloh*
pure	puro	*pooroh*
purple	violeta	*beeohlehta*
purse	el monedero	*ehl mohnehdehroh*
push	empujar	*ehmpoo_h_ahr*
puzzle	el rompecabezas	*ehl rohmpehkahbehthahs*
pyjamas	el pijama	*ehl pee_h_ahmah*

Q

quarter	la cuarta parte	*lah kwahrtah pahrteh*
quarter of an hour	el cuarto de hora	*ehl kwahrtoh deh ohrah*
queen	la reina	*lah reheenah*
question	la pregunta	*lah prehgoontah*
quick	rápido	*rahpeedoh*
quiet	tranquilo	*trahnkeeloh*

R

radio	la radio	*lah rahdyoh*
railways	los ferrocarriles	*lohs fehrrohkahrreelehs*
rain (verb)	llover	*lyohbehr*
rain	la lluvia	*lah lyoobyah*
raincoat	el impermeable	*ehl eempehrmehahbleh*
raisins	las uvas pasas	*lahs oobahs pahsahs*
rape	la violación	*lah beeohlahthyohn*
rapids	el rápido	*ehl rahpeedoh*
rash (skin)	la erupción cutánea	*lah ehroopthyohn kootahnehah*
raspberries	las frambuesas	*lahs frahmbwehsahs*
raw	crudo	*kroodoh*
raw ham	el jamón (serrano)	*ehl _h_ahmohn sehrrahnoh*

143

raw vegetables	las verduras crudas	lahs behrdoorahs kroodahs
razor blades	las hojas de afeitar	lahs o_hahs deh ahfeeheetahr
read (verb)	leer	lehehr
ready	listo	leestoh
really	en realidad	ehn rehahleedahdh
receipt	el recibo	ehl rehtheeboh
recipe	la receta	lah rehthehtah
reclining chair	la tumbona	lah toombohnah
recommend	recomendar	rehkohmehndahr
rectangle	el rectángulo	ehl rehktahngooloh
red	rojo	roh_hoh
red wine	el vino tinto	ehl beenoh teentoh
refrigerator	el refrigerador	ehl rehfree_hehrahdohr
regards	recuerdos	rehkwehrdohs
region	la región	lah reh_hyohn
registered	certificado	thehrteefeekahdoh
relatives	los parientes	lohs pahryehntehs
reliable	fiable/seguro	fyahbleh/sehgooroh
religion	la religión	lah rehleeh_yohn
rent out	alquilar	ahlkeelahr
repair (verb)	arreglar	ahrrehglahr
repairs	el arreglo	ehl ahrrehgloh
repeat	repetir	rehpehteer
report	el atestado	ehl ahtehstahdoh
resent	tomar a mal	tohmahr ah mahl
responsible	responsable	rehspohnsahbleh
rest (verb)	descansar	dehskahnsahr
restaurant	el restaurante	ehl rehstahoorahnteh
retired	jubilado	_hoobeeladoh
retirement	la jubilación	lah _hoobeelahthyohn
return (ticket)	el billete de ida y vuelta	ehl beelyehteh deh eedah ee bwehltah
reverse (vehicle)	dar marcha atrás	dahr mahrchah ahtrahs
rheumatism	el reuma	ehl rehoomah
rice	el arroz	ehl ahrrohth
ridiculous	tontería(s)	tohntehreeah(s)
riding (horseback)	montar a caballo	mohntahr ah kahbahlyoh
riding school	el picadero	ehl peekahdehroh
right	derecha	dehrehchah
right (on the)	a la derecha	ah lah dehrehchah
right of way	la preferencia	lah prehfehrehnthyah
ripe	maduro	mahdooroh
risk	el riesgo	ehl ryehsgoh
river	el río	ehl reeoh
road	el camino	ehl kahmeenoh
roadway	la calzada	lah kahlthahdah
roasted	asado	ahsahdoh
rock	la roca	lah rohkah
rolling tobacco	el tabaco para liar	ehl tahbahkoh pahrah leeahr
roof rack	la baca	lah bahkah
room	la habitación	lah ahbeetahthyohn
room number	el número de la habitación	ehl noomehroh deh lah ahbeetahthyohn

room service	el servicio en la habitación	*ehl sehrbeethyoh ehn lah ahbeetahthyohn*
rope	la cuerda	*lah kwehrdah*
rosé	el vino rosado	*ehl beenoh rohsahdoh*
roundabout	la rotonda	*lah rohtohndah*
route	la ruta	*lah rootah*
rowing boat	el bote de remos	*ehl bohteh deh rehmohs*
rubber	la goma	*lah gohmah*
rubbish	tontería(s)	*tohntehreeah(s)*
rucksack	la mochila	*lah mohcheelah*
rude	descortés/ maleducado	*dehskohrtehs/ mahlehdookahdoh*
ruins	las ruinas	*lahs rweenahs*
run into	encontrar	*ehnkohntrahr*

S

sad	triste	*treesteh*
safari	el safari	*ehl sahfahree*
safe	la caja fuerte	*lah kahhah fwehrteh*
safe/secure	seguro	*sehgooroh*
safety pin	el imperdible	*ehl eempehrdeebleh*
sail	la vela	*lah behlah*
sailing boat	el velero	*ehl behlehroh*
salad	la ensalada	*lah ehnsahlahdah*
salad oil	el aceite	*ehl ahthehyteh*
salami	el salami	*ehl sahlahmee*
sale	las rebajas, la liquidación	*lahs rehbahhahs, lah leekeedahthyohn*
salt	la sal	*lah sahl*
same	mismo	*meesmoh*
same	lo mismo	*loh meesmoh*
sandwich	el bocadillo	*ehl bohkahdeelyoh*
sandy beach	la playa de arena	*lah plahyah deh ahrehnah*
sanitary towel	la compresa	*lah kohmprehsah*
sardines	las sardinas	*lahs sahrdeenahs*
satisfied	contento	*kohntehntoh*
Saturday	el sábado	*ehl sahbahdoh*
sauce	la salsa	*lah sahlsah*
saucepan	la cacerola	*lah kahthehrohlah*
sauna	la sauna	*lah sahoonah*
sausage	el embutido	*ehl ehmbooteedoh*
savoury	salado	*sahlahdoh*
say (verb)	decir	*dehtheer*
scarf	la bufanda (woollen)	*lah boofahndah*
scarf	el pañuelo	*ehl pahnywehloh*
scenic walk	la visita a la ciudad (a pie)	*lah beeseetah ah lah thyoodahdh (ah pyeh)*
school	la escuela	*lah ehskwehlah*
scissors	las tijeras	*lahs teehehrahs*
scooter	la vespa	*lah behspah*
scorpion	el escorpión	*ehl ehskohrpyohn*
scrambled eggs	los huevos revueltos	*lohs wehbohs rehbwehltohs*
screw	el tornillo	*ehl tohrneelyoh*

Word list

15

screwdriver	el destornillador	*ehl dehstohrneelyahdohr*
sculpture	la escultura	*lah ehskooltoorah*
sea	el mar	*ehl mahr*
seasick	mareado	*mahrehahdoh*
seat	el asiento	*ehl ahsyehntoh*
seat	el asiento, la butaca	*ehl ahsyehntoh, lah bootahkah*
second (adj.)	segundo	*sehgoondoh*
second	el segundo	*ehl sehgoondoh*
second-hand	de segunda mano	*deh sehgoondah mahnoh*
sedative	el calmante	*ehl kahlmahnteh*
see (person)	visitar	*beeseetahr*
see	mirar	*meerahr*
self-timer	el disparador automático	*ehl deespahrahdohr ahootohmahteekoh*
semi-skimmed	semidesnatado	*sehmeedehsnahtahdoh*
send	enviar	*ehnbyahr*
sentence	la frase	*lah frahseh*
September	septiembre	*sehptyehmbreh*
serious	grave	*grahbeh*
service	el servicio	*ehl sehrbeethyoh*
serviette	la servilleta	*lah sehrbeelyehtah*
set (verb)	marcar	*mahrkahr*
sewing thread	el hilo de coser	*ehl eeloh deh kohsehr*
shade	la sombra	*lah sohmbrah*
shallow	poco profundo	*pohkoh prohfoondoh*
shampoo	el champú	*ehl chahmpoo*
shark	el tiburón	*ehl teeboorohn*
shave (verb)	afeitar	*ahfeheetahr*
shaver	la afeitadora eléctrica	*lah ahfehytahdohrah ehlehktreekah*
shaving brush	la brocha de afeitar	*lah brohchah deh ahfeheetahr*
shaving cream	la crema de afeitar	*lah krehmah deh ahfeheetahr*
shaving soap	el jabón de afeitar	*ehl hahbohn deh ahfeheetahr*
sheet	la sábana	*lah sahbahnah*
sherry	el jerez	*ehl hehrehht*
shirt	la camisa	*lah kahmeesah*
shoe	el zapato	*ehl thahpahtoh*
shoe polish	la crema de zapatos	*lah krehmah deh thahpahtohs*
shoe shop	la zapatería	*lah thahpahtehreeah*
shoelaces	los cordones	*lohs kohrdohnehs*
shoemaker	el zapatero	*ehl thahpahtehroh*
shop (verb)	hacer la compra	*ahtehr lah kohmprah*
shop	la tienda	*lah tyehndah*
shop assistant	la vendedora	*lah behndehdohrah*
shop window	el escaparate	*ehl ehskahpahrahteh*
shopping centre	el centro comercial	*ehl thehntroh kohmehrthyahl*
short	corto	*kohrtoh*
short circuit	el cortocircuito	*ehl kohrtohtheerkweetoh*

shoulder	el hombro	*ehl ohmbroh*
show	el espectáculo	*ehl ehspehktahkooloh*
shower	la ducha	*lah doochah*
shutter	el obturador	*ehl ohbtoorahdohr*
sieve	el tamiz	*ehl tahmeeth*
sign (verb)	firmar	*feermahr*
sign	el cartel	*ehl kahrtehl*
signature	la firma	*lah feermah*
signposted walk	la excursión	*lah ehxkooresyohn*
	señalizada	*sehnyahleethahdah*
silence	el silencio	*ehl seelehnthyoh*
silver	la plata	*lah plahtah*
silver-plated	plateado	*plahtehahdoh*
simple	sencillo	*sehntheelyoh*
single (unmarried)	soltero	*sohltehroh*
single	individual	*eendeebeedwahl*
single ticket	el billete de ida	*ehl beelyehteh deh*
		eedah
sir	señor	*sehnyohr*
sister	la hermana	*lah ehrmahnah*
sit	estar sentado	*ehstahr sehntahdoh*
size (shoes)	el número	*ehl noomehroh*
size	la talla	*lah tahlyah*
ski boots	las botas de esquí	*lahs bohtahs deh*
		ehskee
ski goggles	las gafas de esquí	*lahs gahfahs deh*
		ehskee
ski instructor	el profesor de esquí	*ehl prohfehsohr deh*
		ehskee
ski lessons/class	la clase de esquiar	*lah klahseh deh*
		ehskeeahr
ski lift	el telesquí	*ehl tehlehskee*
ski pants	los pantalones de	*lohs pahntahlohnehs*
	esquiar	*deh ehskeeahr*
ski pass	el bono (de remontes/	*ehl bohnoh (deh*
	esquí)	*rehmohntehs/ehskee)*
ski slope	la pista de esquí	*lah peestah deh*
	(alpino)	*ehskee (ahlpeenoh)*
ski stick	el bastón de esquí	*ehl bahstohn deh*
		ehskee
ski suit	el traje de esquiar	*ehl trah<u>h</u>eh deh*
		ehskeeahr
ski wax	la cera para esquí	*lah thehrah pahrah*
		ehskee
ski/skiing	esquiar, el esquí	*ehskeeahr, ehl ehskee*
skin	la piel	*lah pyehl*
skirt	la falda	*lah fahldah*
skis	los esquís	*lohs ehskees*
sleep (verb)	dormir	*dohrmeer*
sleep well!	que descanse	*keh dehskahnseh*
sleeping car	el coche cama	*ehl kohcheh kahmah*
sleeping pills	los somníferos	*lohs sohmneefehrohs*
slide	la diapositiva	*lah deeahpohseeteebah*
slip (women's)	la combinación	*lah kohmbeenahthyohn*
slip road	la entrada	*lah ehntrahdah*
slow	despacio	*dehspahthyoh*
slow train	el tren ómnibus	*ehl trehn ohmneeboos*

small	pequeño	pehkehnyoh
small change	el cambio, el dinero suelto	ehl kahmbyoh, ehl deenehroh swehltoh
smell unpleasant (verb)	oler mal	ohlehr mahl
smoke	el humo	ehl oomoh
smoke (verb)	fumar	foomahr
smoked	ahumado	ahoomahdoh
smoking compartment	el departamento de fumadores	ehl dehpahrtahmehntoh deh foomahdohrehs
snake	la serpiente	lah sehrpyehnteh
snorkel	el esnórquel	ehl ehsnohrkehl
snow (verb)	nevar	nehbahr
snow	la nieve	lah nyehbeh
snow chains	la cadena antideslizante	lah kahdehnah ahnteedehsleethahnte
soap	el jabón	ehl hahbohn
soap box	la jabonera	lah hahbohnehrah
soap powder	el jabón en polvo	ehl hahbohn ehn pohlboh
soccer	el fútbol	ehl footbohl
soccer match	el partido de fútbol	ehl pahrteedoh deh footbohl
socket	el enchufe	ehl ehnchoofeh
socks	los calcetines	lohs kahlthehteenehs
soft drink	el refresco	ehl rehfrehskoh
sole (fish)	el lenguado	ehl lehngwahdoh
sole	la suela	lah swehlah
solicitor	el abogado	ehl ahbohgahdoh
someone	alguien	ahlgyehn
sometimes	a veces	ah behthehs
somewhere	en alguna parte	ehn ahlgoonah pahrteh
son	el hijo	ehl eehoh
soon	pronto	prohntoh
sorbet	el sorbete	ehl sohrbehteh
sore	la úlcera	lah oolthehrah
sore throat	el dolor de garganta	ehl dohlohr deh gahrgahntah
sorry	perdón	pehrdohn
sort/type	la clase	lah klahseh
soup	la sopa	lah sohpah
sour	agrio	ahgreeoh
sour cream	la nata ácida	lah nahtah ahtheedah
source	la fuente	lah fwehnteh
south	el sur	ehl soor
souvenir	el recuerdo de viaje	ehl rehkwehrdoh deh byahheh
spaghetti	los espaguetis	lohs ehspahgehtees
Spanish	español	ehspahnyohl
spanner (openended)	la llave (de boca)	lah lyahbeh(deh bohkah)
spanner	la llave de tuercas	lah lyahbeh deh twehrkahs
spare	la reserva	lah rehsehrbah
spare part	la pieza de recambio	lah pyehthah deh rehkahmbyoh
spare tyre	el neumático de reserva	ehl nehoomahteekoh deh rehsehrbah

spare wheel	la rueda de recambio	*lah rwehdah deh rehkahmbyoh*
speak	hablar	*ahblahr*
special	especial	*ehspehthyahl*
specialist	el especialista	*ehl ehspethyahleestah*
specialty	la especialidad	*lah ehspehthyahleedah*
speed limit	la velocidad máxima	*lah behlohtheedahdh mahxeemah*
spell (verb)	deletrear	*dehlehtrehahr*
spicy	picante	*peekahnteh*
splinter	la astilla	*lah ahsteelyah*
spoon	la cuchara	*lah koochahrah*
spoonful	la cucharada	*lah koochahrahdah*
sport (play)	hacer deporte	*ahthehr dehpohrteh*
sport	el deporte	*ehl dehpohrteh*
sports centre	la sala de deportes	*lah sahlah deh dehpohrtehs*
spot/place	el sitio	*ehl seetyoh*
sprain (verb)	torcerse	*tohrthehrseh*
spring	la primavera	*lah preemahbehrah*
square	el cuadrado	*ehl kwahdrahdoh*
square (town)	la plaza	*lah plahthah*
square metre(s)	metro(s) cuadrado(s)	*mehtroh(s) kwahdrahdoh(s)*
squash	el squash	*ehl skwahsh*
stadium	el estadio	*ehl ehstahdyoh*
stain	la mancha	*lah mahnchah*
stain remover	el quitamanchas	*ehl keetahmahnchahs*
stairs	las escaleras	*lahs ehskahlehrahs*
stalls (theatre)	la platea	*lah plahtehah*
stamp	el sello	*ehl sehlyoh*
start (car)	arrancar	*ahrrahnkahr*
station	la estación	*lah ehstahthyohn*
statue	la estatua	*lah ehstahtooah*
stay (lodge)	alojarse	*ahlo<u>h</u>ahrseh*
stay (verb)	quedarse	*kehdahrseh*
stay	la estancia	*lah ehstahnthyah*
steal (verb)	robar	*rohbahr*
steel, stainless	el acero, inoxidable	*ehl ahthehroh, eenohxeedahbleh*
stench	el mal olor	*ehl mahl ohlohr*
sting (verb)	picar	*peekahr*
stitch (med.)	el punto	*ehl poontoh*
stitch (verb)	suturar	*sootoorahr*
stock	el caldo	*ehl kahldoh*
stockings	las medias	*lahs mehdyahs*
stomach	el estómago, el vientre	*ehl ehstohmahgoh, ehl byehntreh*
stomach ache	el dolor de vientre/ estómago	*ehl dohlohr deh byehntreh/ ehstohmahgoh*
stomach cramps	los retortijones	*lohs rehtohrtee<u>h</u>ohnehs*
stools	las heces	*lahs ehthehs*
stop (verb)	parar	*pahrahr*
stop	la parada	*lah pahrahdah*
stopover	la escala	*lah ehskahlah*
storm	la tormenta	*lah tohrmehntah*

straight	liso	_leesoh_
straight ahead	todo recto	_tohdoh rehktoh_
straw	la pajita	_lah pah<u>h</u>eetah_
strawberries	las fresas	_lahs frehsahs_
street	la calle	_lah kahlyeh_
street side	el lado de la calle	_ehl lahdoh deh lah kahlyeh_
strike	la huelga	_lah wehlgah_
strong (tobacco)	negro	_nehgroh_
study (verb)	estudiar	_ehstoodyahr_
stuffing	el relleno	_ehl rehlyehnoh_
subscriber's number	el número de abonado	_ehl noomehroh deh ahbohnahdoh_
subtitled	subtitulada	_soobteetoolahdah_
succeed	salir bien	_sahleer byehn_
sugar	el azúcar	_ehl ahthookahr_
sugar lumps	los terrones de azúcar	_lohs tehrrohnehs deh ahthookahr_
suit	el traje	_ehl trah<u>h</u>eh_
suitcase	la maleta	_lah mahlehtah_
summer	el verano	_ehl behrahnoh_
summertime	la hora de verano	_lah ohrah deh behrahnoh_
sun	el sol	_ehl sohl_
sun hat	el sombrero de playa	_ehl sohmbrehroh deh plahyah_
sunbathe	tomar el sol	_tohmahr ehl sohl_
Sunday	el domingo	_ehl dohmeengoh_
sunglasses	las gafas de sol	_lahs gahfahs deh sohl_
sunrise	la salida del sol	_lah sahleedah dehl sohl_
sunset	la puesta del sol	_lah pwehstah dehl sohl_
sunstroke	la insolación	_lah eensohlahthyohn_
suntan lotion	la crema solar	_lah krehmah sohlahr_
suntan oil	el aceite bronceador	_ehl ahthehyteh brohnthehahdohr_
supermarket	el supermercado	_ehl soopehrmehrkahdoh_
surcharge	el suplemento	_ehl sooplehmehntoh_
surf	el surf	_ehl soorf_
surf board	la tabla de surf	_lah tahblah deh soorf_
surgery	la consulta	_lah kohnsooltah_
surname	el apellido	_ehl ahpehlyeedoh_
surprise	la sorpresa	_lah sohrprehsah_
swallow (verb)	tragar	_trahgahr_
swamp	el terreno pantanoso	_ehl tehrrehnoh pahntahnohsoh_
sweat	el sudor	_ehl soodohr_
sweet	el caramelo	_ehl kahrahmehloh_
sweet	dulce	_doolteh_
sweetcorn	el maíz	_ehl maheeth_
sweetener	la sacarina	_lah sahkahreenah_
sweets	las golosinas	_lahs gohlohseenahs_
swim (verb)	nadar	_nahdahr_
swimming pool	la piscina	_lah peestheenah_
swimming trunks	el bañador	_ehl bahnyahdohr_
swindle	la estafa	_lah ehstahfah_
switch	el interruptor	_ehl eentehrrooptohr_

| synagogue | la sinagoga | *lah seenahgohgah* |

table	la mesa	*lah mehsah*
table tennis	el pingpong	*ehl peenpohn*
tablet	la tableta	*lah tahblehtah*
take (photograph)	sacar	*sahkahr*
take (time)	durar, tardar	*doorahr, tahrdahr*
take (verb)	emplear, usar, tomar	*ehmplehahr, oosahr, tohmahr*
take pictures	fotografiar, sacar fotos	*fohtohgrahfyahr, sahkahr fohtohs*
taken	ocupado	*ohkoopahdoh*
talcum powder	el talco	*ehl tahlkoh*
talk (verb)	hablar	*ahblahr*
tampons	los tampones	*lohs tahmpohnehs*
tap	el grifo	*ehl greefoh*
tap water	el agua del grifo	*ehl ahgwah dehl greefoh*
tart	la tarta	*lah tahrtah*
taste (verb)	probar	*prohbahr*
tax free shop	la tienda libre de impuestos	*lah tyehndah leebreh deh eempwehstohs*
taxi	el taxi	*ehl tahxee*
taxi stand	la parada de taxis	*lah pahrahdah deh tahxees*
tea	el té	*ehl teh*
teapot	la tetera	*lah tehtehrah*
teaspoon	la cuchara de té	*lah koochahrah deh teh*
telegram	el telegrama	*ehl tehlehgrahmah*
telephoto lens	el teleobjetivo	*ehl tehlehohbhehteeboh*
television	la televisión	*lah tehlehbeesyohn*
telex	el télex	*ehl tehlehx*
temperature	la temperatura	*lah tehmpehrahtoorah*
temporary filling	el empaste provisional	*ehl ehmpahsteh prohbeesyohnahl*
tender	tierno	*tyehrnoh*
tennis	el tenis	*ehl tehnees*
tennis ball	la pelota de tenis	*lah pehlohtah deh tehnees*
tennis court	la pista de tenis	*lah peestah deh tehnees*
tennis racket	la raqueta de tenis	*lah rahkehtah deh tehnees*
tennis shoes	los zapatos de tenis	*lohs thahpahtohs deh tehnees*
tenpin bowling	los bolos	*lohs bohlohs*
tent	la tienda	*lah tyehndah*
tent peg	la estaca	*lah ehstahkah*
terrace	la terraza	*lah tehrrahthah*
terrible	terrible	*tehrreebleh*
thank (verb)	agradecer	*ahgrahdehthehr*
thank you	gracias	*grahthyahs*
thaw	deshelar	*dehsehlahr*
the day after tomorrow	pasado mañana	*pahsahdoh mahnyahnah*

Word list

15

theatre	el teatro	ehl tehahtroh
theft	el robo	ehl rohboh
there	allí	ahlyee
thermal bath	el baño termal	ehl bahnyoh tehrmahl
thermometer	el termómetro	ehl tehrmohmehtroh
thick	grueso/gordo	grwehsoh/gohrdoh
thief	el ladrón	ehl lahdrohn
thigh	el muslo	ehl moosloh
thin	fino, flaco	feenoh, flahkoh
things	las cosas	lahs kohsahs
think	pensar	pehnsahr
third	la tercera parte	lah tehrthehrah pahrteh
thirsty, to be	la sed	lah sehdh
this afternoon	esta tarde	ehstah tahrdeh
this evening	esta noche	ehstah nohcheh
this morning	esta mañana	ehstah mahnyahnah
thread	el hilo	ehl eeloh
throat	la garganta	lah gahrgahntah
throat lozenges	las pastillas para la garganta	lahs pahsteelyahs pahrah lah gahrgahntah
throw up	vomitar	bohmeetahr
thunderstorm	la tormenta eléctrica	lah tohrmehntah ehlehktreekah
Thursday	el jueves	ehl hwehbehs
ticket (admission)	la entrada	lah ehntrahdah
ticket (travel)	el billete	ehl beelyehteh
tickets	los billetes	lohs beelyehtehs
tidy (verb)	recoger	rehkohehr
tie	la corbata	lah kohrbahtah
tights	el leotardo, el panty	ehl lehohtahrdoh, ehl pahntee
time (occasion)	la vez	lah behth
time	el tiempo	ehl tyehmpoh
timetable	el horario	ehl ohrahryoh
tin	la lata	lah lahtah
tip (money)	la propina	lah prohpeenah
tissues	los pañuelitos de papel	lohs pahnywehleetohs de pahpehl
toast	el pan tostado, las tostadas	ehl pahn tohstahdoh, lahs tohstahdahs
tobacco	el tabaco	ehl tahbahkoh
toboggan	el trineo	ehl treenehoh
today	hoy	oy
toe	el dedo del pie	ehl dehdoh dehl pyeh
together	juntos	hoontohs
toilet	el water/los servicios/ el lavabo	ehl bahtehr/lohs sehrbeethyohs, ehl lahbahboh
toilet paper	el papel higiénico	ehl pahpehl eehyehneekoh
toiletries	los artículos de tocador	lohs ahrteekoolohs deh tohkahdohr
tomato	el tomate	ehl tohmahteh
tomato purée	el tomate triturado	ehl tohmahteh treetoorahdoh
tomato sauce	el ketchup	ehl kehchoop
tomorrow	mañana	mahnyahnah

tongue	la lengua	*lah lehngwah*
tonic water	el agua tónica	*ehl agwah tohneekah*
tonight	esta noche	*ehstah nohcheh*
too much	demasiado	*dehmahsyahdoh*
tools	las herramientas	*lahs ehrrahmyehntahs*
tooth	el diente	*ehl dyehnteh*
toothache	el dolor de muelas	*ehl dohlohr deh mwehlahs*
toothbrush	el cepillo de dientes	*ehl thehpeelyoh deh dyehntehs*
toothpaste	el dentífrico	*ehl dehnteefreekoh*
toothpick	el palillo	*ehl pahleelyoh*
top up	rellenar	*rehlyehnahr*
total	el total	*ehl tohtahl*
tough	duro	*dooroh*
tour	la excursión, el paseo	*lah ehxkoorsyohn, ehl pahsehoh*
tour guide	el guía	*ehl gheeah*
tourist card	la tarjeta de turista	*lah tahrhehtah deh tooreestah*
tourist class	la clase turista	*lah klahseh tooreestah*
Tourist Information office	la oficina de (información y) turismo	*lah ohfeetheenah deh (eenfohrmahthyohn ee) tooreesmoh*
tourist menu	el menú turístico	*ehl mehnoo tooreesteekoh*
tow	remolcar	*rehmohlkahr*
tow cable	el cable de remolque	*ehl kahbleh deh rehmohlkeh*
towel	la toalla	*lah tohahlyah*
tower	la torre	*lah tohrreh*
town hall	el ayuntamiento	*ehl ahyoontahmyehntoh*
town/city	la ciudad	*lah thyoodahdh*
toys	los juguetes	*lohs hoogehtehs*
traffic	el tráfico	*ehl trahfeekoh*
traffic light	el semáforo	*ehl sehmahfohroh*
trailer tent	el remolque tienda	*ehl rehmohlkeh tyehndah*
train	el tren	*ehl trehn*
train ticket	el billete de tren	*ehl beelyehteh deh trehn*
train timetable	la guía de trenes	*lah gueeah deh trehnehs*
translate	traducir	*trahdootheer*
travel (verb)	viajar	*byahhahr*
travel agent	la agencia de viajes	*lah ahhehnthyah deh byahhehs*
travel guide	la guía	*lah gheeah*
traveller	el pasajero	*ehl pahsahhehroh*
traveller's cheque	el cheque de viajero	*ehl chehkeh deh byahhehroh*
treacle/syrup	la melaza	*lah mehlahthah*
treatment	el tratamiento	*ehl trahtahmyehntoh*
triangle	el triángulo	*ehl treeahngooloh*
trim	cortar las puntas	*kohrtahr lahs poontahs*

trip	el paseo, la excursión	*ehl pahsehoh,lah ehxkoorsyohn*
trouble	la molestia	*lah mohlehstyah*
trousers (long, short)	los pantalones (cortos, largos)	*lohs pahntahlohnehs (kohrtohs,lahrgohs)*
trout	la trucha	*lah troochah*
trunk call	interurbano	*eentehroorbahnoh*
trunk code	el prefijo	*ehl prehfee<u>h</u>oh*
trustworthy	digno de confianza	*deegnoh deh kohnfyahnthah*
try on (clothes)	probarse	*prohbahrseh*
T-shirt	la camiseta	*lah kahmeesehtah*
tube	el tubo	*ehl tooboh*
Tuesday	el martes	*ehl mahrtehs*
tumble drier	la secadora	*lah sehkahdohrah*
tuna	el atún	*ehl ahtoon*
tunnel	el túnel	*ehl toonehl*
turn	la vez	*lah behth*
TV	la televisión	*lah tehlehbeesyohn*
tv and radio guide	la guía de radio y televisión	*lah gheeah deh rahdyoh ee tehlehbeesyohn*
tweezers	los alicates	*lohs ahleekahtehs*
tyre (bicycle)	la cubierta	*lah koobyehrtah*
tyre lever	el desmontador de neumáticos	*ehl dehsmohntahdohr deh nehoomahteekohs*
tyre pressure	la presión de los neumáticos	*lah prehsyohn deh lohs nehoomahteekohs*

U

ugly	feo	*fehoh*
umbrella	el paraguas	*ehl pahrahgwahs*
under	abajo, debajo de	*ahba<u>h</u>oh, dehba<u>h</u>oh deh*
underground railway	el metro	*ehl mehtroh*
underground railway system	la red de metro	*lah rehdh deh mehtroh*
underground station	la estación de metro	*lah ehstahthyohn deh mehtroh*
underpants	los calzoncillos	*lohs kahlthohntheelyohs*
understand	entender	*ehntehndehr*
underwear	la ropa interior	*lah rohpah eentehryohr*
undress (verb)	desvestirse	*dehsbehsteerseh*
unemployed	en paro	*ehn pahroh*
uneven	desigual	*dehseegwahl*
university	la universidad	*lah ooneebehrseedah*
unleaded	sin plomo	*seen plohmoh*
urgent	urgente	*oor<u>h</u>ehnteh*
urine	la orina	*lah ohreenah*
usually	por lo general	*pohr loh <u>h</u>ehnehrahl*

V

vacate	desalojar	*dehsahloh<u>h</u>ahr*
vaccinate	vacunarse	*bahkoonahrseh*
vagina	la vagina	*lah bah<u>h</u>eenah*
vaginal infection	la infección vaginal	*lah eenfehkthyohn bah<u>h</u>eenal*

valid	válido	*bahleedoh*
valley	el valle	*ehl bahlyeh*
valuable	costoso	*kohstohsoh*
van	la furgoneta	*lah foorgohnehtah*
vanilla	la vainilla	*lah baheeneelyah*
vase	el florero	*ehl flohrehroh*
vaseline	la vaselina	*lah bahsehleenah*
veal	la carne de ternera	*lah kahrneh deh tehrnehrah*
vegetable soup	la sopa de verduras	*lah sohpah deh behrdoorahs*
vegetables	la verdura	*lah behrdoorah*
vegetarian	vegetariano	*beh<u>h</u>ehtahryahnoh*
vein	la vena	*lah vehnah*
vending machine	la máquina automática	*lah mahkeenah ahootohmahteekah*
venereal disease	la enfermedad venérea	*lah ehnfehrmehdahdh behnehrehah*
via	pasando por	*pahsahndoh pohr*
video recorder	el video	*ehl beedehoh*
video tape	la cinta de vídeo	*lah theentah deh beedehoh*
view	la vista	*lah beestah*
village	el pueblo	*ehl pwehbloh*
visa	el visado	*ehl beesahdoh*
visit (verb)	visitar	*beeseetahr*
visit	la visita	*lah beeseetah*
vitamin tablets	las tabletas de vitaminas	*lahs tahblehtahs deh beetahmeenahs*
vitamins	la vitamina	*lah beetahmeenah*
volcano	el volcán	*ehl bohlkahn*
volleyball (play)	jugar al vóleibol	*<u>h</u>oogahr ahl bohleheebohl*
vomit (verb)	vomitar	*bohmeetahr*

W

wait (verb)	esperar	*ehspehrahr*
waiter	el camarero	*ehl kahmahrehroh*
waiting room	la sala de espera	*lah sahlah deh ehspehrah*
waitress	la camarera	*lah kahmahrehrah*
wake up (verb)	despertar	*dehspehrtahr*
walk	el paseo	*ehl pahsehoh*
walk (take a)	salir a caminar	*sahleer ah kahmeenahr*
walk (verb)	ir (andando)	*eer(ahndahndoh)*
wallet	la cartera	*lah kahrtehrah*
wardrobe	el guardarropa	*ehl gwahrdahrrohpah*
warm	caliente	*kahlyehnteh*
warn	avisar, llamar	*ahbeesahr,lyahmahr*
warning	el aviso	*ehl ahbeesoh*
wash (verb)	lavar	*lahbahr*
washing (dirty)	la ropa sucia	*lah rohpah soothyah*
washing line	la cuerda de colgar la ropa	*lah kwehrdah deh kohlgahr lah rohpah*
washing machine	la lavadora	*lah lahbahdohrah*
washing-powder	el detergente	*ehl dehtehr<u>h</u>ehnteh*
wasp	la avispa	*lah ahbeespah*

Word list
15

watch	el reloj	*ehl rehlohh*
water	el agua	*ehl ahgwah*
water ski	el esquí acuático	*ehl ehskee ahkwahteekoh*
waterproof	impermeable	*eempehrmehahbleh*
wave-pool	la piscina con oleaje	*lah peestheenah kohn ohlehahheh*
way (means)	el remedio	*ehl rehmehdyoh*
way (on the)	en el camino	*ehn ehl kahmeenoh*
way	el lado	*ehl lahdoh*
we	nosotros	*nohsohtrohs*
weak	débil	*dehbeel*
weather	el tiempo	*ehl tyehmpoh*
weather forecast	el pronóstico del tiempo	*ehl prohnohsteekoh dehl tyehmpoh*
wedding	la boda	*lah bohdah*
Wednesday	el miércoles	*ehl myehrkohlehs*
week	la semana	*lah sehmahnah*
weekend	el fin de semana	*ehl feen deh sehmahnah*
weekend duty	la guardia de fin de semana	*lah gwahrdyah deh feen deh sehmahnah*
weekly ticket	el abono semanal	*ehl ahbohnoh sehmahnahl*
welcome	bienvenido	*byehnbehneedoh*
well	bien, bueno	*byehn, bwehnoh*
west	el oeste	*ehl ohehsteh*
wet	mojado	*mohahdoh*
wet (weather)	lluvioso	*lyoobyohsoh*
wetsuit	el traje de surf	*ehl trahheh deh soorf*
what?	¿qué?	*keh?*
wheel	la rueda	*lah rwehdah*
wheelchair	la silla de ruedas	*lah seelyah deh rwehdahs*
when?	¿cuándo?	*kwahndoh?*
where?	¿dónde?	*dohndeh?*
which?	¿cuál?	*kwahl?*
whipped cream	el chantilly	*ehl chahnteelyee*
whipping cream	la nata para batir	*lah nahtah pahrah bahteer*
white	blanco	*blahnkoh*
who?	¿quién?	*kyehn?*
wholemeal	integral	*eentehgrahl*
wholemeal bread	el pan integral	*ehl pahn eentehgrahl*
why?	¿por qué?	*pohr keh?*
wide-angle lens	el objetivo gran angular	*ehl obhehteeboh grahn ahngoolahr*
widow	la viuda	*lah byoodah*
widower	el viudo	*ehl byoodoh*
wife	la mujer	*lah moohehr*
wind	el viento	*ehl byehntoh*
windbreak	la protección contra el viento	*lah prohtehkthyohn kohntrah ehl byehntoh*
windmill	el molino	*ehl mohleenoh*
window	la ventanilla, la ventana	*lah behntahneelyah, lah behntahnah*